MIND-SWORD

MIND-SWORD
Mastering the Asian Dark Arts of Mind Manipulation

DR. HAHA LUNG

CITADEL PRESS
Kensington Publishing Corp.
www.kensingtonbooks.com

CITADEL PRESS BOOKS are published by

Kensington Publishing Corp.
119 West 40th Street
New York, NY 10018

All Kensington titles, imprints, and distributed lines are available at special quantity discounts for bulk purchases for sales promotions, premiums, fund-raising, educational, or institutional use. Special book excerpts or customized printings can also be created to fit specific needs. For details, write or phone the office of the Kensington special sales manager: Kensington Publishing Corp., 119 West 40th Street, New York, NY 10018, attn: Special Sales Department; phone 1-800-221-2647.

CITADEL PRESS and the Citadel logo are Reg. U.S. Pat. & TM Off.

First printing: Ocotober 2012

10 9 8 7 6 5 4 3 2 1

Printed in the United States of America

ISBN-13: 978-0-8065-3507-4
ISBN-10: 0-8065-3507-5

To Todd "Mr. Machiavelli" Wilson

and

J. J. "Prof. Quiz" Samsa

DISCLAIMER

"The information contained herein is meant to be used for *informational and educational* purposes only." . . . They made us say that. Of course, if you diligently study the "informational" part of this presentation, you will be in a much better position to give your enemies a little "educational" come-uppance the next time they dare raise their hand against you or your loved ones!

Oh, and they also made us say "Don't try this at home." . . . (Instead try these techniques at work with your A-hole boss, and the next time you're trapped at the DMV with that *bee-atch* who you know is deliberately "slow walking" you, and the next time you need to outsmart some would-be car-jackin', pants-saggin', "economically underprivileged" street punk who can quote you the stats, birthday, and jock-strap size of every player on his favorite B-ball team but who can't seem to sit still long enough to get his GED!

We heartily *disclaim* all such people!

Black science: Generic: Any strategy, tactic, or technique used to undermine a person's ability to reason and respond for themselves. Synonyms for mind control and manipulation. Term originally coined by Dr. C. B. Black.

ADDITIONAL NOTE

Portions of this current collection of the craft and cunning of Myamoto Musashi were gleaned in part from Dr. Lung's *Mind Control* (Citadel Press, 2006) and his *Mind Penetration* (Citadel Press, 2007).

CONTENTS

IV. Modern-Day Musashi   *152*

V. 108 Secrets of the Samurai (And a Few New Tricks Even They Never Heard Of!)

MIND-SWORD

INTRODUCTION

"Skill and Skull"

"The mind should not be pulled about by the body;
the body should not be pulled about by the mind."
—Miyamoto Musashi

IT WAS ONCE said of the nineteenth-century philosophy firebrand Friedrich Nietzsche that "before Nietzsche, philosophy was *only* philosophy . . . after Nietzsche, philosophy became *dangerous!*"

Similarly, while there were undoubtedly accomplished Samurai in general and masterful swordsmen in particular in Japan prior to the sixteenth century, none before him, nor any of those who lived after him, ever came close to rivaling the claim to fame of Ben No Soke (1594–1645).

Better known to history as Miyamoto Musashi, here is the man ultimately—*universally acknowledged* by both friend (of whom he boasted few) and foe (of whom he bested many!) as *Kensei,* "Sword Saint," the greatest swordsman to ever live in Japan . . . some claim, *in the world!*

Credit where credit is due. More than a handful of true sword "Masters" lived in Japan both *before* and *after* Musashi. Although *after* Musashi, would-be sword adepts walked with a wee bit more *humility,*

Musashi having given them a higher—some claim, *the highest*—standard to emulate.

Since his death—indeed, even while he lived—many were the *speculations*—*some* informed, some merely superstitious—as to "the source" or "the secret" to Musashi's seemingly magical ability to best any foe.

Musashi personally killed over 1,000 men during his lifetime—over sixty of those in personal duels (the first when Musashi was only thirteen!), the rest he slew while fighting in six different wars.

Best a single opponent, and your enemies might be inclined to dismiss your victory as "dumb luck."

Carving *1,000* notches on your scabbard . . . and "dumb luck" leaves the conversation with tail tucked!

A thousand men—warriors of varying skill levels with varying weapons in hand, but *warriors all*—painted Musashi's victories with their life's blood.

That's a whole lot more than "luck"! Perhaps "the favor" of the Gods, Buddhas, and fierce *Fudo*, who still guard the jewels of the Japanese archipelago?

Or perhaps the obvious? The *requisite* to any success: from an early age, Musashi *worked his ass off* to master his chosen craft—his *calling*.

If you decide Musashi's "secret" was "dumb luck" or that he myopically depended on "the will of the Gods" or some other supernatural succor miserly and arbitrarily doled out by an uncaring universe, then, rather than studying the man and the myth and the methods of Master Musashi, you must remain content to "accept" your lot in life, your assigned place and predestined portion (minuscule though it will be!) of the overcrowded and increasingly arid teats Mother Nature begrudgingly shoves into your crying face!

On the other hand, if we *correctly* determine that—as with *all* Masters of their craft—Miyamoto Musashi's success was due to his deliberate equal cultivations of skill and skull, developing his invincible physical prowess while devoting equal blood, sweat, and tears to the culture of his brain, then we, too, one day determine—*and dare*—to master the Musashi Method, to make it our own.

Whether then, having apprehended Musashi's *Bushido,*we choose to focus our attention on defeating our foe with brilliant blade, blunt force trauma, or a wily bank statement, it matters not. Only victory matters. *That* is the essence—both skill and skull of the Musashi Method.

Many think it ironic, even amazing, that Musashi, "Japan's greatest swordsman," won his greatest duels *without* ever drawing his sword!

A swordsman who so perfected his art to the use of *two* swords, before ultimately reaching the point of perfection to where he no longer *needed* to use a sword? Such a man, myth, and method must surely be worthy of our study?

Surely there is something(s) of benefit to be found somewhere within Musashi's mastery of both his *skill* (first with the sword, and then with every other weapon imaginable at the time!). And, just as important if not more so, his mastery of his *skull*—intelligence, both the innate and the gathered variety.

Study of Musashi—man, myth, and method—thus opens the door for mastery of our own "skill and skull," the one vouchsafing the other.

"Skill and skull," Musashi's twin swords.

"The notion that the pen is mightier than the sword is a fantasy. Try waving a book at the man who comes after you with a machete or a gun. Yet the pen can inform the sword."
—**Lieutenant Colonel Ralph Peters**

I.

Musashi: The Man and the Myth

"Goad your foe into attacking before he is ready, and you will always gain the advantage over him."
—**Kojiro Kinaga, one of Musashi's early instructors**

NOTHING COMES FROM nothing. Nothing exists in a vacuum. Even weeds need the right soil in which to grow.

That Miyamoto Musashi was a *wunderkind* from day one has never been in dispute, neither from friend, nor from foe. And while some biographers insist the babe Musashi just one day picked up a blade and started ridding the world of challengers—he did, in fact, kill his first man at the tender age of thirteen, *tender* by Western standards, that is—the fact is, young Musashi had both the already rich *mythos* of the Samurai class to draw from in general, as well as having been blessed—no other word fits; with having been surrounded by some of the best swordsmen and martial arts instructors of his time.

To his credit, when such instructors and influences were not apparent and immediate, young Musashi deliberately and diligently sought them out.

And, as with all great men—or at least men of notable stature—Musashi seems to have learned as much from his *enemies* as he ever did from his *sensei:*

> Although Musashi claimed to have been self-trained, we can assume that he based his training on the models provided by the most accomplished samurai instructors of the day. —Boyé Lafayette De Mente, *Samurai Strategies*

Here, then, is Lesson Number One:

We learn from Musashi: Never stop learning. Even when someone hands you a *Certificate of Completion, high school diploma,* or even a *Yale sheepskin*, that simply means it's time to *really* start studying.

It's been said, "Chasing after the unfamiliar, we fall to the familiar!" Indeed, most auto accidents happen within, what? Five miles of home?

Likewise, the minute you start thinking you know it all, that there's nothing further for you to learn, that's the very minute one of your enemies (yeah, you *do* have enemies!) who does believe in "lifelong learning" gets the upper hand over you by begging, borrowing, or stealing that singular, surprising piece of information—we call it *intelligence* 'round these parts—you (1) were unaware of, and (2) are therefore now unprepared and unable to defend against.

Having mastered the long sword at an early age—for some a lifelong struggle!—Musashi would go on to master the use of two swords simultaneously, as well as the other popular weapons of his day: the *manriki* chain, the *shuriken* throwing star, archery, spear, and *bo-staff.* Still not satisfied, before the end of his life, Musashi also became a respected calligrapher, painter, sculptor, writer, and master of the *cha-do* tea ceremony.

Nothing exists in a vacuum.

"Knowing Your Environment," first and foremost, means recognizing and taking advantage of any *edge* your environment offers you.

Yes, this means our being willing to seize up a rock or break a limb off a tree when necessary to defend ourselves. But, on a deeper level, "Know Your Environment" means taking advantage of every *opportunity* provided by your environment—and that includes every *opportunity to learn*.

Musashi can be accused of being many things during his life—not all of them flattering! What Musashi can never be convicted of is letting an opportunity pass.

Neither can the charge ever be leveled against him that he allowed tradition, family ties, or his "appointed" station in life to hold him back from "lifelong learning."

For Musashi "lifelong learning" had less to do with *longevity* and more to do with "learning" to guard your own *life*—literally!

Thus we find Musashi learning from his estranged father, from those Samurai around him, from the history and often self-serving *mythology* of his own Samurai class, and then from every Tom, Dick, and Buddha he ran into during his wanderings.

THE COMING OF THE SAMURAI

"The heroes of ancient Japan love and die within their shells of silk and steel."
—M. Yourcenar

Musashi was born in the Japanese Samurai class in 1594, but, during his life, he would go out of his way to study the life and crafts of Japan's other three classes: the merchant, artisan, and peasant. "Learn the ways of all crafts" became one of his maxims, indeed, safeguarding him at various times in his life.

For example, finding himself on the losing side of a battle, forced to "go to ground" while his bloodthirsty enemies literally beat the bushes for him, Musashi was able to fall back on survival skills learned from peasants: how to live off the land, how to find shelter, etc. Later in life, Musashi would master various arts (e.g., calligraphy, sculpting, etc.), skills that not only brought him fame (something he never sought) and also opened doors (an advantage he was keenly aware of).

One often overlooked, or at least ill-understood act of Musashi was his sometimes *carving his* fighting sword out of wood, a most useful skill undoubtedly picked up from some peasant craftsman or the other.

Thus, where other of the haughty Samurai class merely *tolerated* the three lower classes, Musashi went out of his way to learn from the *little people* around him.

The *Samurai* did not begin to emerge as a separate and distinct class in Japan until the eighth century, when a specialized cadre of *knights* recruited from well-to-do families were commissioned by the emperor; called *Kondai* (literally, stalwart youth), these were the first "samurai."

Up until this time, the Japanese army had been composed mainly of spear-wielding foot soldiers. In a break with tradition, these new warriors preferred the sword, not only mastering its destructive potential, but also adopting it. Some might say, "parading it," as the symbol of their unique status.

The single-edged *katana* sword that is today synonymous with the Samurai was invented when a master craftsman named Amakuni, living in the time of Emperor Mommu, A.D. 687–708, divided the original two-edged Japanese-by-way-of-China sword.[1]

Japanese mythology in general and Samurai mythos in particular trace the origin of the Japanese, never *Chinese,* sword back to semi-mythical Prince Yamato, who succeeded in uniting Japan, ancestor of the Yamato line of emperors. Reportedly, Yamato discovered a sword in the tail of a great dragon he slew.[2] This Yamato sword went on to become one of the "Three Treasures," Japan's version of "Crown Jewels."[3]

Finally, in the twelfth century, after centuries of fighting between

---

1. See Ratti and Westbrook, *Secrets of the Samurai.* 1973.

2. FYI: Musashi is credited with slaying the *last* dragon on the Japanese islands. Perhaps a cousin to the very real Kimodo dragon?

3. For the mind control application of "Three Treasures Strategy," see Dr. Lung's *Mind Penetration: The Ancient Art of Mental Mastery* (Citadel Press, 2007).

ambitious Samurai *Daimyo* lords leading powerful families and clans of Samurai, the Minimoto clan was led by eldest son, Yoritomo.[4]

Forcing the emperor to a more ceremonial position, Yoritomo declared himself Japan's first *Shogun* (supreme military leader), in effect establishing rule-by-Samurai for the next six hundred years. By the time of Musashi's birth in 1584, the Samurai were both universally respected *and feared* throughout the Far East.

Between Yoritomo coming to power at the end of the twelfth century and Musashi coming into the world in the middle of the sixteenth century, Japanese Samurai had already honed their killing arts through three hundred years of fighting amongst themselves, in addition to withstanding two attempted invasions by heretofore undefeated Mongols (the first in 1266 and again in 1269).

In 1568 Samurai strongman Oda Nobunaga beat out his fellow rival, Daimyo, to seize command, effectively ending a 150-year period of internecine Japanese slaughter known as "The Age of the Warring States."

Nobunagas's rule was followed by the rule of Midiyoshi Toyotomi, a man as unique in his own way as Musashi, born two years after Hidiyoshi came to power.

Musashi and Toyotomi share something in common: the commonfolk.

As already mentioned, Musashi went out of his way to learn from everyone he came into contact with, regardless of their social rank. It is not too far a stretch to imagine that Musashi may have been inspired in this by the fact that Toyotomi, who ruled Japan as "The Taiko," was *not* Samurai, but had been born a commoner.

Toyotomi spent much of his early life as a *Ninja* thief[5] before graduating to spy, then lieutenant for Nobunaga.

If such a "commoner" could ascend via his own mettle and

---

4. For a complete rendering of Minimoto Voritomo's ruthless mind manipulation strategies for seizing and holding power, see *Lost Arts of War* by Dr. Haha Lung (Citadel Press, 2012).
5. See *The Nine Halls of Death* by Dr. Haha Lung and Eric Tucker (Citadel Press, 2007).

manipulation to become supreme leader of Samurai-dominated Japan, perhaps there was something, perhaps *many* things, a Samurai like Musashi could learn from the "little people."

In modern times, think of the "little people" as all those people you come into contact with each day *but don't notice*: the doorman, that bossy lady at the DMV, the clerk at your "routine" stops along the way during a normal day, perhaps even your housekeeper or even your secretary? All the "little people" you *disrespect* by ignoring, who just might hold a grudge, who just might succumb to your enemy's suggestion on how to "get back at that inconsiderate bastard" . . . *you* being the "inconsiderate bastard" in question.[6]

MUSASHI: THE EARLY YEARS

"What pains a man trains a man."
—*Attila the Hun*

As already mentioned, some biographers continue to insist that Musashi was completely self-taught, a prodigy, born with a sword. No, wait! Born with *two katana* in his hands.

Truth be known, Musashi's father was himself a noted swordsman, master instructor for the powerful Shinman clan. In fact, in his masterpiece *Gorin no sho* ("Book of Five Rings"), written near the end of his life, Musashi signs his name *Shinman Musashi no kami Fujiwara no Genshin*, with clear reference to his family's service to the Shinmen.

So, while perhaps not *born* with literal *katana* in hand, the child Musashi came into this world with his first cries being drowned out by the sound of clashing blades.

How could young Musashi *not* have learned *something* from his

---

6. See "Mastering the Tricks of the 'Little People'" in Lung and Prowant's *Mind Warrior: Strategies for Total Mental Domination* (Citadel Press, 2010).

father, his father's *numerous* Samurai students, perhaps even from shugyosha[7] frequenting the elder Musashi's *dojo.*

Most likely, the boy Musashi, back then known as Ben no Soke and nothing if not observant, learned from *all* these.

Genes being genes, his having come from solid sword-wielding stock to begin with, let alone being raised from birth in a school where swordsmanship was taught, Musashi had both Nature *and* Nurture in his favor. We can easily imagine young Musashi not only learning from any and all examples placed before him, but, given the boy's precocious propensity that would come to pass for his personality in later life, we can also easily imagine him quickly, perhaps easily, surpassing not only his father's students, but soon challenging his father as well.

Not surprising then that Musashi should strike out on his own at an early age. Whether this sudden departure from under his father's thumb came *before* he killed his first man at age thirteen, or because of said killing, we can only speculate.

We do know that by age thirteen Musashi was full-grown, reportedly big for a Japanese. Musashi was also left-handed, which may account for his later ability to master the use of two full-sized *katana*, wielding each adroitly with either hand.

Musashi's later trademark wanderlust manifesting at this early age, added to what must have been increasing estrangement from his father, were both further encouraged by the fact the whole of Musashi's world was staring down into the Abyss of violent change—with the Abyss glaring back!

With the death of "the Terrible Taiko" Hidayoshi Toyotomi in 1603, the powerful Tokugawa clan made their move to seize total power from those still supporting the lost Toyotomi cause and from other ambitious factions. All this bloodshed and jockeying for position came to a head at the battle of Sekihahara, which Musashi fought

---

7. Literally "Swordsmen in Training" who travelled from place to place, deliberately seeking out training, often in the form of formal challenges.

in at the age of sixteen. Unfortunately, Musashi backed the losing side against the victorious Tokugawa. Thus, instead of winning glory, like a thousand other "rebels," Musashi found himself a fugitive, forced to survive out in the wilds while the victorious troops of the Tokugawa hunted down and slaughtered any Toyotomi survivors.

Needless to say, Musashi survived and, never a man to hold a grudge, years later he would find himself in service to the Tokugawa regime, a regime that would successfully rule Japan for next two hundred years.

In 1637, then in his sixties, Musashi fought on the side of the Tokugawa regime against the Christians at the rebellion of Shimabara.

THE WAY OF THE RONIN I:
TASTE THE WIND, RIDE THE WAVE

"As long as you remain ignorant of the true Way, even if you think you are on a sure Way and that you are doing well in accordance with Buddhist laws or in accordance with the laws of the world, you will deviate from the true Way, because you overestimate yourself and your way of seeing is distorted."
—*Miyamoto Musashi*

For much of his life, from the time he killed his first man at age thirteen, Musashi travelled the length and breadth of Japan as a *ronin*.

The word *ronin* literally means "wave man," as in a man, specifically a Samurai, who is unattached to any *Daimyo*. This is analogous to a knight with a king to serve.

Samurai became *ronin* for various reasons: the death of their *Daimyo* or the dissolution of his fief, most often for his having backed the wrong faction in some Samurai squabble or the other.

Until the practice was officially outlawed during the Togugawa Period, loyal Samurai practiced *junshi,* ritual suicide, allowing them to *accompany* their Master into The Void, the most notable account of *junshi* being the oft-told 1701 tale of "The 47 Ronin."

It seems Daimyo Kiro had somewhat of an anger management problem.[8] Well aware of this flaw in his rival *Daimyo*'s personality, Kiro's enemy Asano tricked him into drawing his sword in anger while both were visiting the Shogun. As a result of this breach of etiquette, Kiro was ordered to commit *seppuku*, an order he promptly obeyed.

Everyone then expected Kiro's 47 Samurai retainers to follow him with *junshi*. But, to everyone's surprise, and to their disgrace, all 47 instead chose to become *ronin*.

For the next two years, wherever they went, these 47 *ronin* were scorned as cowards.

However, on the second anniversary of Lord Kiro's death, all 47 of his ronin secretly gathered outside Asano's castle and, before anyone inside realized what was happening, they had breached its walls.

Caught by surprise, Asano's Samurai quickly fell beneath the vengeful blades of the 47.

The next morning, the 47 *ronin* placed the head of Asano on the grave of their lord Kiro and then, one by one, all 47 committed *seppuku,* finally joining their Lord in the Afterlife!

Though the tale of The 47 Ronin was said to take place many years after Musashi's death, much of Musashi's life mirrored the wayward, often impoverished, and even despised life of the *ronin* Samurai.

First, it was usually considered dishonorable to have been dismissed by one's *Daimyo*. Sometimes this came about when financially strapped or else politically ostracized *Daimyo* were forced to "downsize." Other times, Samurai were let go because they had proven themselves useless or untrustworthy. People being pretty much the same then as now, there as here, people just assumed the worst: that the Samurai had been tossed out by his Lord for the latter rather than for the former.

Having been dismissed by one *Daimyo*, some Samurai—for example, those fortunate to receive a recommendation from their former

---

8. See *The Nine Halls of Death* by Dr. Haha Lung and Eric Tucker (Citadel Press, 2007).

boss, or those whose skill and reputation preceded them—would likely find service with another *Daimyo.*

However, for the majority of *ronin,* especially during the Tokugawa Period, pickin's were slim. As a result, some became bullies and highwaymen, taking what they wanted from farmers and from unguarded merchants (thereby contributing to the overall disdain and dread in which *ronin* in general were held).

Other *ronin* hired themselves out as bodyguards, some even as assassins. Several Ninja clans and cliques sprang up from dispossessed *ronin.* Still other *ronin* went to work for *Otokodate,* secretive militiaesque fighting units (aka, *hatamoto-yakko*) financed by various guilds and merchant syndicates, who used them for tasks ranging from guarding merchant caravans to street-fighting against rival merchant syndicates.

Finally, some out-of-work Samurai saw the writing on the wall, i.e., that the Tokagawa regime finally forcing peace between the numerous warring Samurai factions meant that, in the future, there would be less demand for Samurai skills. As a result, many Samurai literally hung up their swords and became farmers, craftsmen, even becoming merchants themselves.

During his life as a *ronin,* Musashi played *all* these roles at one time or another: working for one *Daimyo* or another, fighting for them in wars, often teaching martial arts to their other Samurai, hiring on with merchants to bodyguard men and materials, learning the ways of the farmer, the woodsman, the secrets of craftsmen, including swordsmiths. As already mentioned, he gained a reputation for himself as an artist, as adept with clay and brush as he was performing the tea ceremony.

In later years, speaking from experience, Musashi would admonish his students to "learn the ways of all professions." Indeed, much of Musashi's later strategy and philosophy can be traced to the time he spent "learning the ways of all professions," learning how to handle two swords simultaneously while watching priests beat their ceremonial drum with two sticks, to learning how to correctly "cross at the ford" from apprenticing with friendly ferrymen. By the time of his death in 1645 Miyamoto Musashi was universally acknowledged as *Kensei*, "Sword Saint," the greatest swordsman ever to live in Japan, an accolade he has yet to share with another.

That Musashi should ultimately succumb to, of all things, death from natural causes[9] is perhaps the single most amazing aspect of his amazing, some would say, "amazingly *violent*" life. But like warriors everywhere, perhaps warriors in every time, Musashi was not so much violent by nature as he was a man nurtured by violent times. As such, he did not so much contribute to the violence of his time, as he did ride the wave.

The most convincing testimony to Musashi's skills of survival in general, as well as his mastery of Japanese *bujutsu* martial arts in particular, is the fact that despite his *thousands* of life-and-death, kill-or-be-killed encounters, Musashi still managed to die of old age.

Fortunately for us, two years before his death Musashi took the time to write down his thoughts, tactics, and techniques in his *Gorin no sho* ("A Book of Five Rings"). Though written over four hundred years ago, Musashi's *Gorin no sho* remains one of the greatest classics on warfare ever written, easily spoken of in the same breath as Sun Tzu's *Ping Fa* ("Art of War").

At the ripe old age of twenty-two, Musashi had written *Enmei-ryu Kenpo* ("Sword Technique of the Enmei School"), twenty-two lessons of swordsmanship. Then, in 1641, four years before penning the *Gorin no sho*, he wrote the *Hyoho Sanju Go Kajo* ("35 Instructions on Strategy").

Less known, after penning the *Gorin no sho,* Musashi also wrote the smaller *Dokkodo* ("21 Ways to Be Followed Alone"). But today, Musashi's "A Book of Five Rings" remains his master opus.

Far from being some archaic manual on medieval Japanese *kenjutsu* (swordsmanship), Musashi's *Gorin no sho* gifts us with the twin blades, *appreciation and application*, giving us an appreciation of Musashi's bat-

---

9. Best guess, throat cancer.

tlefield insights, as well as a practical application of his tried 'n' true (as opposed to tried 'n' died) strategies, both equally applicable to any and all other areas of endeavor we might decide to undertake.

Modern-day Japan, from businessmen to sports figures, politicians to priests, policemen to *Yakuze* gangsters, consult their always-within-arm's-reach, dog-eared copy of the *Gorin no sho* on a daily basis.

Musashi's *Gorin no sho*'s insightful strategies and incisive tactics are as much head-games as they are head-taking!

Mom was right! "Sticks and stones may break your bones, but words will never harm you." True. Words can't kill you . . . but words *can get you killed.*

Likewise, words devoid of action are only hot air.

One very popular Musashi tale illustrates how action trumps words.

> On the eve of a great battle, Musashi was suddenly called away from making preparations, back to his present *Daimyo*'s tent. Entering the tent, Musashi was disturbed to find the *Daimyo*, whom he knew to usually be a calm, rational man, now visibly upset. "We must call off the battle and withdraw immediately!" the *Daimyo* told Musashi. "My astrologer has just predicted my death tomorrow!" His eyes narrowing, Musashi told a nearby guard, "Summon the astrologer." No sooner did the astrologer arrive than Musashi confronted him. "You say our Lord will die tomorrow?" "The stars have decreed it," announced the wizard
>
> "And when do these stars say *you* will die?" Musashi asked. "Oh, my horoscope says that I will live a long life, that I will have many . . ." Before the astrologer could complete his statement, Musashi's sword had separated the wizard's head from his shoulders. As the wizard's head rolled to a stop at the *Daimyo*'s feet, Musashi

bowed deeply before exiting the tent. The next morning, the *Daimyo*, Musashi at his side, easily won the battle.[10]

In some versions of this tale, the astrologer is later discovered to have been an enemy agent, specifically sent to undermine the *Daimyo*'s confidence. Ironically, such a ploy qualifies as "Cutting at the Edges," a ploy near and dear to Musashi's heart.

"Cutting at the Edges" is simply hitting an opponent where you can, when you can. In *Kenjutsu* this means, when you can't hit your opponent with a telling strike, you content yourself with striking a non-vital target, maiming and bleeding (weakening) him until you can deliver the *coup de grace.*

In Black Science, "Cutting at the Edges" is used when you are unable to attack a rival directly, in which case you undermine his *support network* by attacking those near and dear to him, thereby *bleeding off* his resources, weakening him, making him more vulnerable to your future attack directed at him.

Thus, it's not enough to just "talk the talk." Somewhere along the way you're gonna have to put up or shut up. Some other gunslinger (or swordsman, as the case may be) *is* gonna try your hand, and that's when you'll be forced to "walk the walk" . . . or tuck tail and *run* like hell!

For Musashi, "walking the walk" often meant fighting to-the-death duels, where "appreciation" for martial arts in general and mastery of *Kenjutsu* in particular was forced to manifest itself as practical application, where fate and prior study quickly separated the quick from the dead.

Young Musashi paid his dues. Keep in mind that before he was "Sword Saint," he was just one of many "sword pilgrims" roaming the

---

10. At one time or another, this cautionary tale is found in the Far East associated with everyone from Sun Tzu to Toyotomi to Musashi. As with many things "Eastern," the *lesson* is more important than the *location.*

land, *ronin* in search of food, a little fondling, and a way to improve their fast draw:

> Before the Tokugawa Period very few swordsmen were able to lift the art of the samurai sword on to a higher philosophical plane. The men who succeeded were the *kengo* (master swordsmen) like Myamoto Musashi who went on "warrior pilgrimages" (*musha shugyo*). This was much akin to the common Japanese practice of making long religious pilgrimages to distant parts, thereby obtaining spiritual enlightenment through endeavour and personal discomfort.
>
> The typical *sword pilgrim* was likely to have had some service to a *daimyo* and some battle experience behind him before setting off. His wanderings could last for several years, and might include temporary spells of military service and some teaching. —Stephen Turnbull, *The Samurai and the Sacred*[11]

From lowly *ronin* to praised *kensei* is a long and arduous path indeed, a path that demanded Musashi learn not only to "taste the wind" but also to "ride the wave."

For a *ronin*, for any warrior, for that matter, to "taste the wind" means to always stay alert, figuratively and literally, to which way the wind is blowing, be those winds likely to affect you (1) personally, (2) socially/politically, (3) militarily/self-defense-wise, or (4) financially.

This means learning to spot Mr. Trend and Mr. Trouble *before* they come barreling around the corner with blood in their eye!

If you can train yourself to spot trouble coming soon enough, and you can, then trouble might never catch you having to barricade (and booby-trap) the front door—or else spot you ducking out the back door!

The latter, that "better part of valor," echoes Sun Tzu's ideal that

---

11. See also "Musashi's Zen" later in this chapter.

if our legs aren't long enough to *outrun* trouble, then we at least need to become practiced at *tripping* trouble up at the starting gate, preferably before he ever hears the starter pistol. Better still, pay the man with the starter pistol (conveniently replaced with the *real deal*), to point it in your opponent's direction. To wit:

> Like the "art of war" manuals written by Sun Tzu, the fabled military master of ancient China, Musashi's strategies and tactics are based on deep insights into human nature combined with an uncommon level of pragmatism. His precepts about fighting and succeeding in any endeavor provide valuable lessons for anyone facing challenging circumstances—from the military and business to athletes and the "warriors" of everyday life.
> —Boyé Lafayette De Mente[12]

Ever imagine that you can smell rain coming? You can! But what you're really smelling is *gibberellin,* an oily substance plants secrete in response to changing air pressure, designed to protect them from harsh rain.

Also, ever notice how, when walking toward the ocean, you smell the salt air long before you crest that final dune to actually look out over the water?

In the same way, veteran sailors "taste the wind," smelling (more *feeling* it on their skin) subtle changes in air pressure. This sensing mixed with their previous experience in similar situations tell them, "Aye, 'tis a foul blow a'brewin', mates!"[13]

Ever heard of "pheromones"? Those are the "subconscious" scents mammals, including human beings, give off when aroused or otherwise excited.[14]

---

12. De Mente, 2005: 28.
13. Shrinks call this "operant conditioning."
14. See "Using Their Sense of Smell" in Lung and Prowant's *Mental Dominance* (Citadel Press, 2009).

Down through the centuries, some shadowy Far Eastern cadres have gone to great lengths to train their operatives to fully employ all five senses, to the point where non-initiates often mistook these adepts' mastery of their five senses for a mystical "sixth sense."[15]

On a daily basis, whether we are *conscious* of it or not, we watch each others' *normal* body language. This is why we often feel a vague discomfort that "something's not right," noticing either consciously or subconsciously that another person's body language is "wrong," that there's something "out of the ordinary," often our first *warning* that they're "up to no good."

Trust *paranoia.* . . . It evolved millions of years before *politeness!*

In the same vein, again, whether we're conscious of doing it or doing it unconsciously, we listen carefully to others' "shadow language"—Freudian slips, or something they're going out of their way to leave out of the conversation.[16]

On a larger scale, it's vital that a military commander, businessman, stock broker, and intelligence operative keep abreast of real-time intelligence so as to instantly and consistently adjust their "game plan" to account for the shifting winds of circumstance and flux.

As any surfer will tell you, "You gotta taste the wind before you can ride the wave."

Musashi would concur.

"Ride the Wave" means first and foremost going with the flow. There's a time for "fight" and there's a time for "flight." Why? Because Mother Nature says so.

When the other guy's army is bigger than your army, and you're fresh out of Hannibals and Pattons, it's time to go guerrilla on his ass:

---

15. For a complete course in welding your five senses into a "sixth sense," see "Ying Gong Senses Training" in Dr. Lung's *Mind Penetration: The Ancient Art of Mental Mastery* (Citadel Press, 2007).

16. See "Methods of Mayhem/The Art of Listening" in Dr. Lung's *Mind Control: The Ancient Art of Psychological Warfare* (Citadel Press, 2006).

- Refuse to face him toe-to-toe. Who chooses the battlefield chooses the victory!
- Melt into the background. (Make yourself less of a target, making the enemy pass you by, until the time comes to show him who you are.)
- Bury your dead and bind your wounds. (Metaphorically, this means discarding past plans, plans that obviously *haven't worked* up to this point, and *heal* any bruised egos. Ruthlessly cut loose any ass-kissing "yes" men, resource-sucking *hangers-on,* and/or potential backstabbing turncoats. Better the scalpel now than the sword later.
- Collect and conserve ammunition. (Get *two* of everything, men and material. Best case scenario: Take what you need from your enemy.)
- Gather intelligence. (You need both the *innate variety* of intelligence people are born with. It's vital you seek out and surround yourself with such people, and just as vital, you need to constantly update your information. Whether in business, on the battlefield, or even in the bedroom, out-of-date information will not suffice. In addition to some basic born-with intelligence of your own, you need *gathered intelligence,* current information on your enemy's motives and movements.)
- When ready, take swift and appropriate action. (Yeah, this might be a good time to *reread* what should be by now your dog-eared copy of Sun Tzu.)

In the same way the sailor sways with the roll of the deck beneath his feet, riding the waves, even as his feet remain firm on deck, as with the sailor, so with the *ronin.*

Curiously, while the Samurai *ideal* was to have two equally armed, equally trained warriors fighting toe-to-toe, the *reality* of history shows how, time and again, Samurai, like any savvy warrior cadre who survived long enough for history to take note of them, were always looking for an *edge* over their enemies.

This is why Musashi spent his life travelling the length and breadth of Japan in a lifelong quest dedicated to mastering both conventional and unconventional styles of fighting. You may recall this is what Chinese masters call *cheng* and *ch'i*, direct and indirect methods of engaging your enemy.[17]

Musashi could, if he chose, go *cheng* toe-to-toe with the best of opponents, and he often did. But Musashi was also the undisputed master of the indirect *ch'i* attack. That's why, ironically, Japan's "Sword Saint" defeated his greatest opponents not with his sword but with weapons other than the sword.

Ever on the alert for that one trick[18] that would give him the upper hand, Musashi first mastered the traditional *katana* long sword, before then going on to master the use of *two* full-sized swords simultaneously.

Still not satisfied, Musashi continued to perfect his martial arts by mastering all traditional Samurai weapons: the bow, the spear, the *jutte*,[19] and so on. He then went on to master "forbidden" weapons more associated with the Ninja: the *manriki* fighting chain, the *kusari* sickle, and *Kakushi-jutsu*, the *Ninja* art of fighting with small, easily concealed weapons, e.g., *shuriken* throwing stars.[20]

By the end of his bloody career, Musashi had successfully defeated opponents with every conventional Samurai weapon of his day, quite a few "Ninja" weapons, and even by wielding unexpected and unconventional "Environmental Weapons," such as an empty sword scabbard, a tree limb, a cart, even a kitchen ladle!

Still, no matter what tool he held in his hand, Musashi defeated his

---

17. See "Ping-Fe Kung-Fu" in Lung and Prowant's *Mind Assassins: The Dark Arts of the Asian Masters* (Citadel Press, 2010).

18. Tricks well-mastered are called "techniques." Techniques half-learned are merely "tricks" (*Shihan* Peter Gilbert).

19. An iron baton with a hook on the side (think "The Club") for catching and locking on to attacking swords. Favored by police during the Tokugawa period, Musashi's father was an expert with this weapon, in addition to his sword mastery.

20. See *Classical Budo* by Donn F. Draeger (Whitehall Press, 1973).

foes first and foremost with his "Mind-Sword," using *yuku mireba*, the power to *see* into the heart of his enemy, perceiving and then playing on emotional weaknesses they themselves often do not suspect, such as their overconfidence, their confusion, and their susceptibility to the Five Warning F.L.A.G.S.[21]

Yuku mireba is how Misashi learned to "Taste the Wind." Having "tasted the wind," Musashi could then "Ride the Wave," choosing the path of least resistance, swimming *with,* rather than fighting *against,* the current, using any tactic and any available weapon, *cheng* or *chi*, to win.

The Japanese call this *Masakatsu.* To win by any means necessary.

As with the *ronin* Musashi, so with us. We must learn to "Taste the Wind" and "Ride the Waves," discerning trouble before it has a chance to camp out on our front lawn, doing whatever it takes to safeguard that and those we treasure.

While a few of us might be "rolling stones," most of us won't have the *luxury* in life Musashi *enjoyed* being a *ronin*, with little responsibility other than safeguarding his own head.

Musashi travelled light throughout his whole life. Even during those times he was sedentary, serving one *Daimyo* or another, he still claimed few possessions.

Musashi lived inside his head. But unlike Musashi, few of us can just "hit the road" any time we'd like. Most of us have family and friends who depend on us. Many of us have a spouse and children we're responsible for. (Can you say "deadbeat dad"?)

So how, then, are we in the modern day to *apply* our *appreciation* for Musashi's "Way"?

"Way" capitalized refers to the Japanese suffix *do,* referring to specific techniques and responsibilities within any specific art of lifestyle, e.g., *kendo* = the "Way" (technique, requirements) of the sword (*ken*).

Whereas we'll stick out like a sore thumb (not to mention risk arrest!) if we decide to sport a pair of Samurai swords in our belt,

---

21. Fear, Lust, Anger, Greed, and Sympathy.

Musashi's medieval "Mind-Sword" is available to all of us for use in our daily lives.

What does this "Mind-Sword" consist of?

First, *Masakatsu!*[22] Doing whatever it takes to survive and prosper.

On the physical level, faced with a physical threat, this means we borrow from Musashi's big black bag of dirty tricks any rock, stock, dirt-in-the-eye, or other handy tactic and tool it takes for us to survive and safeguard our loved ones.

Faced with a *mental* attack, e.g., an insult you can't let pass, a non-physical threat, you respond with any of a thousand tried-'n'-true "Black Science"[23] plots and ploys designed to hobble, hoodwink, and otherwise hornswoggle your enemies into submission.

For Musashi, any confrontation, whether precipitated by a tight fist or a loose mouth, held the realistic possibility of someone dying. Yet our trials and tribulations in today's world can be just as treacherous, albeit more subtle, "smile in your face and stab you in the back" holding just as much potential to turn out fatal.

Scenario: That schmuck in the cubicle next to yours has a plan to (1) make you look bad, thereby (2) getting you fired so there will be an opening for his brother.

How devastating would unexpectedly losing your job, perhaps after falsely being accused of some impropriety (e.g., theft, sexual harassment, etc.) be for your family? At the very least we're talking less food on the table. But what about losing your *children's health care?*

That's why, when studying Musashi, we must adapt the attitude, the mind-set, he lived with each day of his life: *to do whatever is necessary to survive and then to prosper.* Just *"surviving"* isn't enough. Cockroaches "survive." Men must aim higher.

Thus, after the *ronin* Musashi teaches us how to "Taste the Wind"

---

22. Always written with an exclamation point.

23. Black Science: generic: Any strategy, tactic, technique, or tool used to undermine a person's ability to reason and respond for themselves. Synonym for mind control and manipulation.

(i.e., increase our overall awareness) and then how to "Ride the Waves" (i.e., go with the flow while adapting to shifting circumstances), we will then learn from Kensei Musashi the *determination* needed to take on and complete any task, any course of learning, achieve any goal.

Musashi's attitude of indomitable determination is called "Crossing at the Ford."

THE WAY OF THE RONIN II: MUSASHI CROSSES AT THE FORD

"Musashi's main strength, as he said many times, was not in superior ability with weapons, but in using his mind to defeat his opponents. And it is obvious that at a very early age he trained his mind as vigorously as he did his body."
—Boyé Lafayette De Mente

Hopefully by now you've realized that people are pretty much the same everywhere. Nor, despite what we'd like to believe, have people changed much in significant ways since ancient times.

In the East, as in the West, there is much dispute about a great many things, some arguments earth-shaking in their implications, some not worth the spit.

Whether in the East or in the West, Shanghai to South Philly, disagreement can be found on any street corner, any time of the day or night. This is because East or West, it's always been easier to disagree than it is to dig up proof.

But in the East, and among those knowledgeable in the West, there is no disagreement as to what are the two greatest treatises ever written on the subject of warfare: Sun Tzu's *Art of War* and Musashi's *A Book of Five Rings.*

Though no specific mention is made, we can rest assured that Musashi studied Sun Tzu, whom the Japanese call *Sonshi.*

Like Sun Tzu, during his violent life Musashi dealt with warfare on several levels at various times. For example, both men knew the one-on-one taste of battle, Sun Tzu from having risen through the ranks the hard way, Musashi from both his sixty-plus one-on-one duels and from his experience as a foot soldier.

In addition, both men knew the demands of command: Sun Tzu from his numerous battlefield campaigns, Musashi from acting as advisor to one *Daimyo* or another.

However, when reading the grand opus of each man, novices often have trouble discerning when Sun Tzu and Musashi are talking strategy (the big picture) or tactics (on-the-ground); when they are talking literal, physical attacks and counters; and when they are speaking figuratively in more psychological, even metaphoric terms.

The answer is: *It's all the same!*

If you're looking for "philosophy," you can certainly find it in both Sun Tzu's *The Art of War* and in *A Book of Five Rings*. If, on the other hand, you're looking for practical, pragmatic, in-your-face-so-I-can-rip-your-face-off (!) advice, you'll find that too.

Whether confronting a foe face-to-face or else plotting a more psychological attack against him, *attitude is still all.*

In *A Book of Five Rings*, when Musashi refers to "attitude," he really is talking about how one holds one's sword in order to block and counterstrike, e.g., "high altitude" (sword held horizontal at forehead level); "low attitude" (sword point held forward and down—designed to entice an opponent).

But "attitude" also means just that: your "attitudes" (mind-set) toward what is taking place.

It was shortly before the end of his life in 1645 that Musashi retired to a cave where he sat in solitude writing his masterpiece, *Gorin no sho*, so called because it is organized into five sections, each named after the traditional Eastern way of reckoning the basic components of life: Earth, Air, Fire, Water, and Void.[24]

According to noted Musashi translator Victor Harris, *A Book of Five*

---

24. Also called "Metal" in China.

Rings is unique among martial texts in that it deals with "both the strategy of warfare and the methods of single combat in exactly the same way."

Or as Musashi himself puts it:

> In my strategy, one man is the same as ten thousand, so this strategy is the complete warrior's craft.

But as straightforward as Musashi himself seems to be, interpretations of Musashi, both the man and his writings, are myriad. In fact, there's seemingly no end to the number of Musashi commentators, ranging from the mystical and the philosophical, to how to use Musashi's tactics to get ahead in the financial world.

Admittedly, *A Book of Five Rings*, like all such works, lends itself to a variety of interpretations. This makes Musashi's instruction "sweet in the mouth, but bitter in the belly," i.e., easy to talk about, but difficult to translate into practical *application*. Even those with a deep appreciation for Musashi still find practical, modern-day *application* for his medieval tactics and techniques elusive. Let alone trying to succinctly sum up the Sword Saint's overall teachings!

Fortunately, we need only look closely[25] in order to discover that Musashi has cunningly done this for us: summing up his philosophy in a succinct and penultimate lesson.[26]

Musashi called this "Crossing at the Ford," a lesson found in the *Fire* section of his *Gorin no sho*.

"Crossing at the Ford" encapsulates the whole of Musashi's strategy for facing life and death in general, and for overcoming enemies in particular, preferably without ever having to draw your sword:

"Crossing at the Ford" gives us the key, actually, *twelve* keys, for honing our Mind-Sword to a fine edge, before then turning that scalpel-like focus toward our enemy. Says Musashi:

---

25. Not just to *look* but to *see*. Remember? *Yuku mireba*, the power to see deeply.

26. "Penultimate" because *death* is always the final lesson.

> I believe this "crossing at the ford" occurs often in a man's lifetime. It means setting sail even though your friends stay in harbor, knowing the route, knowing the soundness of your ship and the favor of the day. When all the conditions are met, and there is perhaps a favorable wind, or tailwind, then set sail. If the wind changes within a few miles of your destination, you must row across the remaining distance without sail.

Even a cursory examination of this paragraph shows it oozing to overflowing with the spirit of determination.

A *ford* is the shallower part of a river or strait between islands, familiar to mariners in general, as well as to a well-travelled *ronin* like Musashi whose wanderlust took him to all corners and all ports of call on the many islands of the Japanese archipelago.

Musashi's words drip with determination to cross to that far shore whatever it takes, in the face of rising foul weather, no matter the desertion by fair-weather friends.

But beyond this obvious interpretation, those who dive deep enough will discover precious pearls of (deliberately hidden?) wisdom.

Thus, "Crossing at a Ford" demands we dare delve deeper.

Says Musashi, "I believe this 'Crossing at a Ford' . . ."

1. It occurs often in a man's lifetime.

Opportunities happen every day. Trouble is, it's human nature that we all too often only see those things we go looking for.

Opportunity doesn't just knock once, even twice. . . . Opportunity is *pounding* at our door continuously, but we're usually too busy bitchin', itchin', and twitchin' to take notice.

Chance favors the prepared mind. A mind is prepared through learning. Learning opens doors. One of them, that same door *opportunity* keeps trying to kick in.

Granted, *opportunity* knocks differently at different times. This requires that we:

- **Pay attention to life!** What's that great Dr. Lung line you just can't stop repeating to all your friends? "Pay attention now . . . or pay the *Undertaker* later."
- **Stop complaining and start campaigning!** Hate to break the news to you, Hoss. But the Universe doesn't know you. Sure, you've got all those earth-shaking ideas, but until you find a way to get them (and yourself) noticed, so far as the Universe is concerned, you're *not* a *star*, you're just a *statistic*!

First you gotta figure out *what* exactly it is you're selling, and then you have to hit the campaign trail just like a politician. Hit every whistle-stop. Never tire of tooting your own horn. Decide what "office" you're running for, e.g., billionaire, power broker, star maker? Whatever! Then *fight for it*! Make the Universe notice you. Squeaky wheel gets the grease, remember?

When you campaign for yourself, you're also campaigning for all you believe in and for all you love. When *you* win, *everybody* you care about benefits.[27]

Tell the truth: Has *anyone* ever made it out of your ghetto neighborhood? Has anyone born up your hillbilly holler ever made it past sixth grade? Got out, and done good?

Sure, they have. If they "made it out," what's *your* major malfunction, numb-nuts? Sure, you can believe they were *born special* or any other excuse you want, just so long as it allows you to remain sitting there on your ass suckin' up Cheetos, playin' video games, and refusing to learn how to spell "library." When opportunity does knock, you'll never be able to hear it over your video game!

Sure, you were born in a ghetto or a trailer park, but how many

---

27. Don't make Dr. Lung tell you "The Last Can of Beans" story again . . .

other kids just like you *did* pay attention in school? How many kids from the same neighborhood *did* graduate, did get some military or vocational skills under their belt? How many of them are doing well? How many of them became the kind of *success story* you wish you could be?

You still can.

Oh, so many excuses, so little time! Read "Ten Good Excuses . . . but Not One Good Explanation!" in Lung and Prowant's *Mind Warrior* (Citadel Press, 2010).

According to Musashi, both *Necessity* and *Opportunity* occur many times in a man's life.

There *will* be times when you're gonna have to "man up," take responsibility, maybe even the lead.

Sometimes this *challenge* comes about because of *Necessity*. Shit happens. And when shit happens, somebody needs to grab hold of a shovel while everyone else is still standing around holding their noses.

Other times, it's *Opportunity* knocking that makes you decide it's time—here and now—to chance "crossing at the ford," to brave those churning waters in order to seize your share (and maybe just a little more!) of what *prize and pride* waits on that far shore.

Musashi promises, or warns, that the time to act, whether trying to outpace *Necessity* or else catch up to *Opportunity*, will occur many times during your life. We need only seize *Opportunity* by the throat once in order to better our lot in life, to ensure that *Opportunity* learns his lesson never to pass our door without at least stopping by to say hello.

2. It means setting sale even though your friends stay in the harbor.

Peer pressure isn't just confined to the playground. Even as adults we often feel the need to conform to family expectations, social norms, and even racial and cultural traditions. It's hard enough to screw up

your courage, swallow your fear, and gird up the ol' loins when deciding to take the path less travelled, to set off on your own without the
blessing of family, friends, and the local shaman. This difficulty is made
even more so depending on how many timid and cynical naysayers you
have to dodge or else drag along behind you on your journey.

All too often we are held back by *toxic* relationships. Some of these
relationships we choose: our jobs, or social and sexual entanglements.
Other codependent, even parasitic relationships are thrust upon us by
birth: familial obligations, perceived and then perpetuated racial limi-
tations,[28] even cultural and nationalistic obligations.[29]

Even those who care about us the most, family and friends, those
who truly have our *best interest* at heart, are often guilty of discourag-
ing us from following our dreams, guilty of holding us back, of telling
us how we should just give up *that crazy and dangerous dream* of trying
something new before we end up in the Poor House. I've got news for
you, my friend: if this is the kind of advice you're getting from those
living under the same roof . . . then you're already living in the Poor
House!

Okay! You've forced Dr. Lung to tell you "The Last Can of Beans"
story again . . .

> The Apocalypse has overtaken you and your family. You,
> your complaining wife, and your two little hungry chil-
> dren are doing your best to survive in your burned-out
> basement.
> Amongst the debris, you find your last can of beans.
> *Who* eats the beans?

Now a whole lot of social conditioning will tell you, "Give the
beans to the children." You might even give half to the old lady just to
stop her kvetching!

---

28. What used to be called "racial stereotypes."
29. Arjuna's dilemma in the *Bhagavad-Gita*.

Either way, that's what all those wolves scratching at that barricaded basement door are hoping you'll do.

What *should* you do?

What you *must* do is eat that last can of beans yourself.

You have to stay strong in order to fight off the wolf pack—be it four-legged or the much more dangerous *two-legged* variety!

You have to be strong enough to stay strong. Strong enough to put up with the sound of your children crying (so long as they are still crying, at least they are still alive), and the sound of your old lady's incessant complaining.

You're not going to be able to do your family, or yourself, any good *unless you first make yourself strong.*

A bunch of weak-minded dorks can't accomplish anything without someone to coordinate them. Lock twelve stupid people in a room and they will not suddenly grow a brain. Ever heard of O.J. Simpson?

Likewise, get 300 million people together and, just 'cause you call it "democracy," that don't mean the man (or woman) best qualified is gonna be sworn in come January. That's because Democracy measures "PR" not "IQ."

Just because everybody and their mother (and maybe your mother too!) are against you, that doesn't mean you're wrong. History is full to overflowing with men (and women) who were told, "You can't do that!" and "That'll never work!" The ones who didn't succumb to all this naysaying are the ones who now *fill* those history books. Gone and forgotten are the mindless millions upon millions who *went along to get along*, who bit their tongues and buried their dreams in the hope that the cruel hand of their fellows would not slap them back into *their place.*

If you fear your fellows . . . then they're not really your *fellows*, are they?

Bottom line: You can't help others unless you first help yourself. Sometimes you *have* to eat the last can of beans. Sometimes, as Musashi tells us, you have to set sail while your friends are still in harbor—still hesitating, or else dead-set against the venture.

It's called egoism,[30] and it's not a bad word. It simply means you're not much good to anyone else until you first get your own house in order.

3. It means knowing the route.

In any serious undertaking, you first gather intelligence, then you formulate a plan, and then, if you're smart, you formulate a "Plan B"—"B" for *backup*.

Gathering background information *and* up-to-date (as current as possible) information is not meant to discourage you. Quite the opposite. The more you know about the people, places, and things that may enhance or else interfere with your mission, the more the likelihood of your success.

At first glance, you might think discovering they've added a couple extra guards on that payroll shipment is a *bad thing*. Look on the bright side. They probably added more guards because there's *more money* to guard!

That's called "spin." And there are people on Madison Avenue *and* in Washington, D.C., who get paid big bucks to do that very thing. Right, they're called "Spin Masters."

Hopefully, you will not be dependent upon some Spin Master (or Spin-meister, if you really want to show off!) for your useful and real-time intelligence gathering, as Spin Masters tend to deal in the *other* direction when it comes to worthwhile intelligence—both the innate and the gathered variety.

You can bet Musashi studied everything he could about his opponents before dueling them. This, in addition to his *innate* and *deliberately developed* "*yuki mirebe* sense," gave him the edge he needed to win every battle.

---

30. Not to be confused with "*egotism*." Get some Max Stirner under your belt. Also read "The Sloth, The Quest, and Becoming a Better Walker" in Dr. Lung's *Mind Control: The Ancient Art of Psychological Warfare* (Citadel Press, 2006).

During the course of any battle, challenge, negotiation, etc., there will be times when you'll be tempted to deviate from your game plan. There will also be times when you *should* deviate from your game plan. Still other times, you will be *forced* to deviate from your initial plan, and this is where "Plan B" comes into play.

"Knowing your route" means knowing:

- *Where* you want to get to (i.e., physical destination, financial destination, successful manipulation of someone's mind-set, etc.).
- *Why* you want to get there (i.e., what do you hope to obtain by going from Point A to Point B, be it a physical destination, financial goal, breaking a bad habit, etc.).
- *What* resources do you need to beg, borrow, or steal[31] in order to accomplish your goal?
- *When* can you expect to accomplish your goal (i.e., what time table are you laboring under?); and,
- *Who* can you reasonably expect to help or hinder your progress?

4. It means knowing the soundness of your ship.

"The sword is the soul of the warrior. If any forget or lose it he will not be excused."
—*Tokugawa Iayasu (1516–1543)*

A craftsman is only as good as his tools, a warrior only as good as his weapons.

The fact that Musashi was forever alternating weapons, from single sword to two swords to no sword to that tree limb over there! testifies to the truth that Musashi's greatest weapon (as well as ours) remains the *Mind-Sword*.

---

31. Musashi's.

Before undertaking any project, investment, venture, or journey, take a realistic accounting of your needs, balancing them against the resources—men and materials—you have at your disposal.

Only a fool sets sail in a leaky boat. This holds true whether we're talking literally or metaphorically.

Dot the "I's," cross the "T's," double-check the tally at the bottom of the page. . . . And always carry a spare life preserver.

And I'm sure you're smart enough to realize that "checking the soundness of your ship" includes checking the "soundness" of your crew? The most worthy of vessels have been scuttled by untested and untrustworthy crews both scurvy and mutinous.

5. It means knowing the favor of the day.

In the *Zandokan* Budokai,[32] the first lesson a student learns is "The Three Knows":

- Know yourself.
- Know your enemy.
- Know your environment.

Having steadfastly set your determination toward "Crossing at the Ford," hopefully you've already realistically taken a full accounting of your own abilities and resources, sidestepped all the naysayers standing in your way, and double-checked the readiness of your ship and, when applicable, your "crew."

But you also need to check which way the wind is blowing— figuratively and literally.

Does the current—and *projected*—environment (physical environment, as well as social/political environment) support this bold and

---

32. School of martial arts founded by *Shihan* Peter Gilba.

innovative course of action you are proposing? Or are you and your novel thoughts and actions fated to frighten and challenge the status quo?

Is the present mentality of your peers (a vital part of any "environment") ready to accept the changes your actions may cause? Can the current marketplace (also part of the "environment") handle your new product? Indeed, is there a market or even a willing ear favoring your bold new invention or innovation?

Finally, what roadblocks in the form of *real enemies* inhabit your present environment and/or any new environment you are either venturing into or else trying to create? How far will such enemies—call them "competitors" if it makes you feel safer—go to prevent you from upsetting their apple cart?

If only to be on the safe side: take what *you* would do in their place, i.e., if you felt your livelihood or way of life was being threatened . . . and then *double* it by factoring in their desperation.

Make a final realistic assessment of your resources and you're *realistically* prepared to call into play. This is what's called a "reality check," what veterans—like Musashi—call a "final weapons check" before embarking on a mission.

Just make certain your "reality check" is just that, based in *reality* and not based on *really-like-it-to-be* wishful thinking.

6. It means knowing there is perhaps a favorable wind, or a tailwind.

It's always better to have the wind at your back than to try spittin' into it. Then again, running against the wind does make you stronger.

A "favorable wind" is another way of saying *carpe diem*, seize the opportune moment, when the wind is fair and confidence high.

Facing uncertain winds, a good sailor changes his *tack*, zigzagging *into* a challenging wind with a firmer grip on the rudder. The lesson:

faced with unfavorable conditions, always be willing to persevere, perhaps change your *tact*.

7. Then set sail.

"Great events hang by a thread. The able man turns everything to profit, neglects nothing that may give him one chance more; the man of less ability, by overlooking just one thing, spoils the whole."
—*Napoleon*

Just do it. There comes a time to either "put up or shut up."

Change is hard. And there'll always be plenty of people standing around laughing at you when you fall flat on your face, even a couple of them who'll try tripping you up if you're not paying attention.

So *don't* fall flat on your face!

The taste of *not trying* is twenty times more bitter in your mouth and a hundred times more gravel in your gut than trying your best, and failing, could ever be.

It's been said, "Experience is what you get when you don't get what you wanted." By the same token, *excuses* are what you give because you (1) *didn't try,* or else (2) *didn't try hard enough.* (Yeah, Dr. Lung comes from that "No Excuses School.")

Taoist Masters tell us that "the journey of a thousand miles begins with a single step." This, Musashi understood:

Step by step walk the thousand-mile road. . . . Study strategy over the years and achieve the spirit of the warrior. Today is victory of yourself of yesterday; tomorrow is victory over lesser men.

8. If the wind changes . . .

"The rule is 'The ability to gain victory by changing and adapting according to opponents is called genius.'"
—Liu Ji (1311–1375)

It's been warned time and again that "no battle plan survives first contact with the enemy."

Ever alert, we adjust, we adapt, and we adopt new ways of thought and action as circumstances and flux demand—no matter whether the contest we're waging is taking place on the battlefield, or in the board room, or in the bedroom. Ultimately the prize goes to the one more adept at reading the other person—be it a rival general, a general manager, or your generally-a-pain-in-the-butt girlfriend!

Victory requires vigilance and the ability to quickly change from nodding your head "Yes!" to shaking it "No!" without giving yourself whiplash.

Adapt or die. We've advanced to the point where we are now able to spindle, fold, and mutilate quite a few of Mother Nature's rules.

"Adapt or die" remains nonnegotiable.

9. Within a few miles of your destination . . .

Most auto accidents happen within a few miles of home, when we relax prematurely.

A relaxed enemy is either (a) *really confident, perhaps even overconfident*, or else (b) *relaxed because you've helped relax him.*

> The beginning is easy, the middle is dangerous, and after the middle, the danger increases further. —Musashi

Musashi was noted (or is that "notorious"?) for lulling his foes into a false sense of confidence, encouraging them to relax—right before he dropped the other shoe—or sword, as the case may be.

Often Musashi would deliberately show up late, long after his opponent(s) had relaxed, having convinced themselves that Musashi had chickened out. Other times Musashi would deliberately lower his sword (as if it had suddenly become too heavy), and/or yawn, knowing that his yawn would soon be mirrored by his opponent.

The game isn't won until the gold is in the bank and your enemy's head is on a silver platter.

The number-one rule of master manipulator and Zen guru entrepreneur *extraordinaire* Robert J. Ringer is "Get Paid!"[33]

The end is important in all things. How many times have we seen the once "great and famous" suddenly brought low later in years by scandal? Nixon? O.J.?

On the other hand, look at those who live remarkably unremarkable lives, but when Fate demanded it, stepped up to the plate and swung for the bleachers? The passengers and crew of 9/11's Flight 93, Captain Sulley.

10. You must row across the remaining distance . . .

Remember that "Plan B" we mentioned earlier? Having committed yourself, your resources, perhaps even your allies and their resources, not to mention those who've trusted you to lead them to victory . . . *stay the course!*

Full effort is full victory. We win by trying.

> Once you have made up your mind, stick to it; there is
> no longer any *if* or *but*. —Napoleon

Fair weather friends, promised funds that never materialize, men and materials that arrive late if at all . . . When the wind no longer favors and fills your sails, you're gonna have to (a) *favor yourself* (Yeah! That "Last Can of Beans" thing again!), and then (b) *fill your hand* with

---

33. See "Looking Out for Number One: Bring in the Ringer!" in Lung and Prowant's *Ultimate Mind Control* (Citadel Press, 2011).

oars and start rowing for all you're worth—*literally*, for all you're worth!

11. Without sail.

Worst-case scenario: Your friends and family have abandoned you, refusing to take part in your "*foolishness*." Your resources have been stretched to the limit, perhaps even to the point of bankruptcy.

In other words, the once-friendly wind has turned against you, or worse still, left you completely, trapping you in the doldrums *sans* succor.

Now you are alone, wondering what to do. . . .

What *do* you do?

You stand alone.

And you *row* on, alone.[34]

And what should you expect as your reward for having dared venture out in the face of the threatening storm of scorn, both hands firm on the tiller, both eyes locked on the prize of that far shore?

If you have to ask, you've booked passage in the wrong boat.

> Among would-be Samurai in Japan, the martial skills were highly prized, but even more prized was the presence of mind. —Lyman and Scott (1989)

Miyamoto Musashi is credited with founding the *Nito-ryu,* the "Two Swords School," having mastered the skill of fighting with the full-sized *katana* at the same time.

Likewise, his "Crossing at a Ford" not only advises us how to persevere, honing our determination, sharpening our will, but this paragraph also "hides" twelve keys for manipulating our foes by exploiting their innate weaknesses.

---

34. Read Hemingway's *The Old Man and the Sea.*

THE WAY OF THE RONIN III: MUSASHI'S ZEN

"Despite his claim that he took nothing from the Buddhist scriptures or any of the other teachings of the day, Musashi's outlook on life was pure Zen, which teaches how to recognize and deal with reality in a detached, objective way—minus the emotions that make life such a trial for so many people."
—Boyé Lafayette De Mente, 2005

Miyamoto Musashi's life reads like one long *musha shugyo*, a warrior's pilgrimage, in effect, wandering from place to place learning when you can, teaching when you must, perfecting your *Bushido*.

Today, *Bushido*, the "Way" of the warrior, is permanently fused with *Zen*, that ever-elusive, esoteric branch of Buddhism.

Of course, Zen being Zen, we could argue that Zen is in no way either "elusive" nor "esoteric." Quite the opposite, Zen has made a reputation for itself as the simplest, non-adorned branch of Buddhism. ·

But, as with many things Eastern, Eastern philosophy in particular, Zen can be interpreted and apprehended on a myriad of levels. But, rather than add to a neophyte's confusion, this actually extends the possibility of our *experiencing* Zen on *all those levels* . . . as did Musashi.

First, a little background on the origins of Zen.

Remember that flower The Buddha (c. 500 B.C.) held up in lieu of his final sermon eagerly anticipated by disciples?

Only Kashyapa understood the significance of this "silent sermon." Thus, Buddha's *final* sermon is considered the *first* "Zen" sermon. *(More on this in a minute.)*

But no sooner did the newly arrived Bodhidharma[35] inform the prideful emperor that no matter how many fine temples and golden Buddhas you order built, it doesn't bring you one step closer to enlightenment, than the emperor banished Bodhidharma from the Imperial Court.

---

35. Bodhidharma is called *Tsmo* in China, and *Daruma* in Japan.

But rather than return to India[36] Bodhidharma settled near Loyang, China, at a humble Taoist temple named for the "small forest" where it was located: *Shaolin*.

Legend has it that, still not satisfied with his accumulated Buddhist wisdom, Bodhidharma spent his first nine years at Shaolin in deep meditation facing a wall.

To stay awake, legend is convinced Bodhidharma pulled out his eyelashes one-by-one. And where each of these eyelashes fell, there sprang up a tea plant. That's why, to this day, the *Cha-do* tea ceremony is one of the most recognized and respected "meditative" practices of Zen.

FYI: Musashi was a *Master* of the tea ceremony.

Eventually, through "wall-gazing," Bodhidharma experienced *Nirvana,* a word that in Indian-Sanskrit literally translates to "blowing out the fire," i.e., extinguishing all unnecessary desire, "desire" being the Buddhist boogeyman.

Before long, Bodhidharma began teaching this successful meditation technique to his Shaolin brethren.

In India, Bodhidharma's meditation technique was known as *dhyana.* In China they called it *Shan* (also written *Ch'an*), a word the Japanese pronounce *Zen.*

Bodhidharma's *Shan* was less concerned with the *appreciation* of Buddhist scripture, more concentrating on the *application* of your ass to your meditation mat!

A well-loved, oft-told *Zen* teaching tale illustrates this:

> One day an exasperated young student came to his Zen Master's chamber and declared firmly, "I'm quitting!"
>
> "Any particular reason?" his Master asked. "I became a student of Zen so I could learn the secrets of the Universe but, instead, I'm all confused by all the different religions and various philosophies in the world."

---

36. A prophet goes where he is needed most . . . and welcomed!

"Come here, knucklehead,"[37] said the Master, leading his student to an open window. "Do you see that *mountain* over there? I want you to imagine all those different religions, all those various philosophies as just different *paths,* all leading up the mountain. Some of those paths are smooth and easy to walk. Other paths are difficult, with shrubs and big boulders blocking the way. Some paths are straight, some very crooked. Some wide, others very narrow . . . but *all* of them lead to the top of the mountain."

"Ah!"smiled the student. "Now I see! All the different religions, all the varying philosophies, all of them are trying to get to the top of the mountain! And *our Zen* is just another way up the mountain." "No, dumbass!"[38] sighs the Master, whacking the student hard on the back of his head.[39] "Our Zen *is* the mountain!"

As with most things "Zen," this story lends itself to several interpretations. Is the Master merely being a smart-ass (as Zen teachers are prone to be)? Is the student really that dense (as Zen students are prone to be)?

After all, the student *did* pick up on what the Master was telling him: *all* spiritual paths, indeed, end at the same summit (or at least should). Ah! But even when the student ascends to *this initial level* of understanding, the Master is always nearby, ready to ensure that, instead of the student smugly congratulating himself for his "enlightenment," a swift smack to the head (figuratively and often *literally!*) will keep the student at least pointed and plodding in the direction of *the next level.*

---

37. Loose translation.

38. Again, loose translation.

39. It is traditional to whack whoever you're telling this story to at this point. It's okay. It's a "Zen thing."

In case you haven't figured it out by now, Musashi and Zen have a lot in common. . . . *Neither ever rest(ed) on their laurels.*

Thus, no matter how many hours spent in meditation, no matter how many days and weeks and months spent trying to make sense of the latest *koan* riddle given you by the Master ("What the hell *is* the sound of one hand clapping?"), rest assured there will always be yet another level of understanding to scale *until* the Zen student finally understands, realizes, is enlightened to the fact that it's the process, the path, *the "doing,"* that's most important to focus on.

How did those great Western Zen musicians, Aerosmith, put it? Life's a journey not a destination.

What was the first, last, and only technique taught by Bodhidharma? *"Sit!* Just sit and meditate . . . no matter how long it takes. Just sit." In Japan they call this *Zazen.*

While "Just sit!" might be the only *meditation* technique Bodhidharma taught his Shaolin brothers, as all martial arts students know, he also taught them something just as valuable . . . how to stay awake. And then how to use the same techniques to put their enemies to sleep!

The story goes that, seeing his Shaolin brethren falling asleep during marathon meditation sessions, Bodhidharma taught them *yoga*-like exercises designed to strengthen them both physically and mentally: a three-part training regimen composed of *Ying Gong* (body-toughening calisthenics), *Chi Gong* ("internal organ strengthening"), and *Jing Gong* (meant to increase a student's overall awareness via the full use of all five senses).[40]

The "calisthenics" Bodhidharma taught the monks soon strengthened them to the point where, when the temple monastery was besieged by bandits, the brothers of Shaolin were able to beat the ban-

---

40. For a complete training course on these Shaolin training techniques, see "The Rise and Fall of Shaolin" in Dr. Lung's *Mind Penetration* (Citadel, 2007), and "Six Senses: Ying Gong and Jing Gong" in Lung and Prowant's *Mental Dominance* (Citadel Press, 2009).

dits back after Bodhidharma revealed that his "calisthenics" were, in fact, derived from Indian martial arts!

Those movements later became known (and feared) as "the 18 Hands of Lo-Han" (*Lo-Han* meaning "monk"), and became the basis for all the *Kung-fu* fighting styles that followed.

Musashi could be the poster boy for Zen, as the two have so much in common.

Like Zen, Musashi was/is, at first glance, simple, unassuming . . . often (it was complained!) *unwashed.*

As with Zen's "Just sit!", so, too, Musashi was a simple vagabond, a *ronin,* making his living from hand to mouth.

And like Zen, with its aggravating *koan* riddles and Gary Larson-esque[41] two-dimensional one-panel conundrums, what at first appears simple, even nonsensical, suddenly (Aha!) reveals hidden layers of meaning designed to enlighten us.

Like Zen, Musashi never stopped looking for those "deeper levels" of perfection and, like Zen, finally realized somewhere along the path up the *mountain* that the path mattered little, it was *the mountain* that was all important.

All that is fine and dandy, you say, but how do *I* apply what you're telling me to the "real" world?

Simply put, keep pushing against your walls, keep testing the limits of your world. Nietzsche. Ayn Rand. Does Dr. Lung *look* like a librarian to you?

You know how all the underachievers complain how "some people are never satisfied"?

Be one of those people! Musashi was.

In very Zen-like fashion, he never seemed satisfied with his current level of achievement, not in the martial arts, nor in the other scholarly and craft-arts he undertook to master.

Somewhere along the path Musashi came to the Zen-like revela-

---

41. Greatest living Zen Master.

tion that "perfection" was not some ever-receding-into-the-distance goal to be chased, some summit of a mystical *fujiyama* never to be reached. Rather, he realized "perfection" **was** the path, a daily striving to be better than yesterday. Thus he tells us: "Today is victory over yourself of yesterday: tomorrow is your victory over lesser men."

And so, for Musashi, mastery of one sword led to mastery of two swords, then to the "Mind-Sword" of *No-sword,* to mastery of all conventional Samurai *and* Ninja weapons, to the using of whatever "Environmental Weapon" presented itself, to, ultimately, his swearing off the killing of others—at worst, wounding and chasing them away, at best, ignoring them altogether.

Can we credit the study of Zen for this "enlightenment" in Musashi?

Recall how Musashi advises us to "study the Ways of all professions." Is it not then logical Musashi himself would have at least familiarized himself with the tenets and philosophies current to his time—if only in order to assess their potential for trouble?

According to some sources, Musashi went much further than a superficial glance at Zen:

> Musashi obviously mastered the Zen way of meditating, and attributed much of his success in battle and in the arts to simple practice. —De Mente (2005), 48

Another school of thought argues that Musashi's "Zen" wasn't actually "Zen" from the Zen school of Buddhism but, rather, simply an outgrowth of an even older Samurai tradition:

> His [Musashi's] Zen was godless. It was the Zen of the old samurai warriors who meditated to perfect their breathing and most of all their sword stroke. —Kosko (1993), 200

Of course, this in itself would be "Zen." Ironically, to give something (or someone) the label "Zen" would make it just a little less "Zen." This harkens back to an ancient Taoist saying, the first line of the Taoist "Bible," the *Tao Te Ching,* that "the *Tao* that can be spoken is not the true *Tao.*"

Musashi may have been "Zen" before the Japanese even knew what Zen was!

While Buddhism arrived in Japan somewhere around the middle of the sixth century, the Zen branch didn't officially make landfall until Japanese monk Eisai (1141–1215) returned from studying Bodhidharma's teachings in China. Eisai founded the *Rinzai* school of Zen, which relies heavily on the use of Master-Disciple dialogue and *koan* riddles to help the student "break through" the mundane, to experience the true nature of existence hidden beneath.

In turn, Eisai's successor, Dogen (1200–1253), is credited with founding the *Soto* school, which, in keeping with Bodhidharma's original teaching, emphasizes *Zazan* meditation. According to Dogen, even meditation on simple (the simpler, the better!), everyday objects could bring about realization.

Eisai is also credited with introducing the drinking of tea to the *Shogun* of Kamakura. Curious, given that age-old tale about Bodhidharma's plucked eyelashes becoming tea plants. Significant, in that the *cha-do* tea ceremony (which Musashi took time to master) is another practice now intricately connected to Zen.

Right from the start, Zen fit many Samurai like sword to scabbard. So much so that today, Zen is the philosophy most associated with the Samurai. This, despite the fact that many Samurai of Musashi's time and after embraced the native *Shinto,* other more "esoteric" schools of Buddhism, and even Christianity.

In examining why some Samurai so readily bonded with Zen, one noted writer lists the virtues "manliness," "honest poverty," "courage," and "composure of mind" that Zen and Bushido had in common.[42]

Oftentimes even those Samurai who practiced Shinto and Christianity still added Zen meditation to their routine and regimen . . . anything to gain an added edge.

---

42. See *The Religion of the Samurai* by Kaiteen Nukariya, 1913.

For example, Musashi contemporary Kamiizumi Nobutsuna of the Kashima Shin school of *kenjutsu,* though a Shinto practitioner, also studied Zen, as did his student Yagu Muneyoshi.

Likewise, Muneyoshi's son Yagu Munenori (1529–1606), master student of the *Shinkage* ("New Shade") school,[43] studied Zen meditation under the famous Zen priest Tauan (1573–1645).

What we in the modern day need to keep in mind is that the Zen of Musashi's time was different—more *immediate*—than it was in later years, when the absence of dire threat gave Samurai more time to "contemplate" the Universe:

> When samurai were real fighting men the value they attached to Zen could be very different. The "means" provided by *Zazen* was an excellent "training for the mind," and would therefore be a very valuable preliminary exercise for the fight. —Turnbull (2006), 146

Turnbull explains how "by the blending of self and weapon through action" the swordsman moves toward "complete emptiness," which he sees as the aim of all Zen practice.

However, Turnbull goes on to point out that most of the classic writings on Zen would not come about until many years after Musashi was already "walking the walk, talking the talk":

> One must always bear in mind, however, that most of the written material about Zen and Swordsmanship was produced at a time when the art of the samurai swordsman was not encumbered by any need to actually win battles. By being thus concerned with means rather than ends, sword-fighting entered the realm of meditation on daily things that would have been so valued by Dogen. —Turnbull (2006), 146

---

43. Founded by sixteenth-century Master Kamizumi Hidetsuna. For more on the strategy of Kamizumi Hidatsuna, see Lung and Prowant's *Mind Manipulation* (Citadel Press, 2002).

Musashi's *life* follows this same pattern: moving from practical, actual street-fighter—the *Zen* of the street, if you will—to his foreswearing off killing as he perfected his art in later years. And, in classic "wandering monk" style, he spent the last few years of his life literally living, meditating, and writing in a cave.

Whatever the chronology of Musashi's "Zen" (chicken or the egg?), five very *Zen*-like principles of winning stand out in both Musashi's life and in his philosophy.[44]

Little Buddha, Big Buddha

According to the classic text *Zenrin*: "Taking up one blade of grass, use it as a sixteen-foot golden Buddha."

This again harkens back to The Buddha's "single flower" sermon.

Recall that Chinese Taoists maintain that a single energy comprises the whole of the Universe, *chi*. Mysteriously, there is the same *amount* or *degree* of *chi* in a mountain as there is in a single grain of sand. Hence, it stands to reason, Taoist reasoning, that there isn't all that much difference between a blade of grass and a golden Buddha statue.

But how do we, let alone a master swordsman like Musashi, apply this concept?

Musashi himself explained how, starting out to make a 100-foot statue of The Buddha, you first make a *model* statue, perhaps only a foot high. Thus from a small *pattern*, great things may emerge.

By the taking of single steps, we eventually discover we have travelled a thousand miles.

This is the basis for Musashi's declaration that fighting and winning a battle against one man is the same as fighting and winning against ten million men.

Memory experts call this "chunking." When you have a lot to remember, a phone number for instance, divide it up into more manageable "chunks" of three and four numbers.

---

44. For what good is a philosophy if it is not reflected in one's life?

Musashi's tactic of "Cutting at the Edges" follows this same principle: Unable to break through an enemy's sword defense to get to a vital organ, cut him on the arm, on the leg, *anywhere and everywhere* your weapon can touch, wearing him down. Go guerilla.

Likewise, in Black Science strategy, when we are unable to attack an enemy directly, we get at him through one of his close associates, a friend, family member, his secretary.

Depending on his secretary to "watch his back" during an important presentation, your businessman enemy is chagrined to find himself having to go it alone because his secretary had to take off work and go to the police station to bail out her son who just happened to get caught with a sizable bag of controlled substance in his glove compartment that he swears to Jesus and all the Saints he has no idea in hell how it got there!

Or, "Cutting at the Edges" goes hi-tech and . . . somehow . . . your rival's office hard drive suddenly gets wiped clean, along with that vital report the boss was waiting for.

From little ideas grow great innovations. Conversely, small weeds, left unattended, destroy a whole garden.

Learn from All

This includes all nouns: people, places, and things.

In his *Gorin no sho*, "The Scroll of Wind" section, Musashi tell us:

> You cannot know with certainty the way of your own
> school without knowing the *Way* of others.

This is practical advice, whether we're talking a one-on-one sword duel, or a high-stakes board room negotiation. The more you know about the other "school," the better your chances of:

1. *Not* being surprised by them.
2. Coming up with a few surprises of your own that they never see coming!

Musashi improved his *swordsmanship* by watching *Kodo* drummers adroitly wielding their thick batons.

Ever on the alert for the least little thing he could learn from *anyone,* this is why Musashi ordered his students to "learn the *ways* of all professions" . . . *all professions,* because you never know what might become useful . . . or deadly.

FYI: Did you know the (in)famous four-pronged Ninja *senban-shuriken* ("throwing star") was derived from a simple carpenter's nail-pulling tool? Likewise, those traditional martial arts weapons—*nunchukes, sai, tonfa*—all were once simple farm and fishing implements.

And while *people* should never be used as "tools," admittedly, they have similar uses: getting hammered, getting screwed!

Even the least of students has something to teach the Master. Learn from all. Musashi did.

> The point here is that individuals should continuously strive to increase their knowledge and improve themselves in a comprehensive, holistic way. Musashi emphasized that success in one field or area contributes to success in other fields—an insight that is often ignored in today's world. —De Mente (2005), 92

Transcend Technique

Musashi warned us against having a "favorite weapon," lest we give the enemy a chance to develop a counter. Extrapolating: this means not being predictaable in any way.

We remain (or become) unpredictable by, first: deliberately varying routes and routine, by suspending "tradition" in favor of favorable winds and fortuitous fords.

Second, we become unpredictable, often without consciously realizing it, by *transcending* normal tactics and technique. In Zen, this is the point and place where all the parts of our long periods of practice mysteriously "gel," becoming greater than the sum of those parts:

Technical knowledge is not enough. One must transcend technique so that the art becomes an artless art, growing out of the unconscious. —Zen Master Takuan

Thus we find ourselves face-to-face with the epitome (never *stereotype*!) of the Zen warrior:

A Zen sword-player may stand in an almost nonchalant attitude before the foe as if the latter can strike him in any way he liked; but when he actually tries his best, the Zen man would overcome him with his very unconcernedness. —*The Awakening of Zen* by D. T. Suzuki (1987)

Such "transcendence," when witnessed by non-initiates, often appears "magical" and mysterious, leading to tales of fantastic derring-do by Zen adepts in general and Samurai Zen "Masters" in particular.

Things are not what they seem . . . nor are they otherwise.

This line from the Buddhist *Lankavatara* sutra (scripture) reflects the sometimes contradictory nature of Zen in general and its founder, Bodhidharma, in particular.

Many people have a hard time wrapping their mind around the idea that Buddhism, a religion dedicated to *ahimsa* ("harm no one"), was also the religion of choice for sword-carrying Samurai whose lives were anything *but* peaceful. And, keep in mind, Bodhidharma himself was somewhat of a contradiction, again a Buddhist Master who, nonetheless, is also considered the *grandfather* of all Eastern martial arts.

Not surprising, following in this same "Zen" tradition, Musashi also appears to us a somewhat contradictory figure: his father a well respected Sword Master and instructor in his own right, young

Musashi could have easily taken over the "family business" and lived life as your average Samurai.

Not to be.

Having mastered the sword (as well as any other weapons he could literally get his hands on), Musashi then first foreswore killing, and then discarded fighting altogether. Not your typical Samurai behavior. Musashi is obviously not what he seemed . . . but then, neither is he otherwise.

This verse from the *Lankavatra sutra* is meant to keep Zen students from becoming too "full of themselves."

As Sun Tzu warns: "We are never in so much danger as when we are *cocksure of ourselves.*"

Overconfidence has gotten far more people killed than *under-confidence* ever did.

Consider: if a person has doubts about their ability to accomplish a task, they will either (1) avoid that task (thereby cutting down their chances of failing, possibly to the point of fatality!), or else (2) they'll sojourn on with the task, paying especial attention (thereby, again, cutting down their chances of somehow getting blindsided).

So *"Things are not what they seem"* . . . someone tells us this (or our gut instinct tells us this) and, what? Right. *We'd pay better attention.*

". . . Nor are they otherwise." It is what it is. Deal with reality. Make realistic observations of your enemies' abilities and assets, as well as your own abilities and assets (or lack thereof), and then use those realistic observations ('round these parts we call that "intelligence gathering") to help you craft realistic battle plans.

"Nor are they otherwise" also warns us against taking the enemy at face value. His job is to confuse us. Our job is to see through his smokescreen.

On the practical side, Musashi shows up at a duel armed, not with *katana,* but rather with a crudely carved wooden sword. His enemy now breathes an inner sigh of relief, since his enemy, Musashi is not armed with a *lethal* weapon.

Ah, but "things are not what they seem. . . ."

Musashi kills his opponent with one blow from his simple wooden weapon.

". . . Nor are they otherwise!"

Like Sun Tzu, Musashi realized that we are never in as much danger as when we are overconfident: overconfident in our mastery of *one* weapon. Thus Musashi's insistence that we favor no single weapon, leading by his own example as he mastered *all* weapons!

> Nothing whatever is hidden; from of old, all is clear as daylight. —The *Zanrin*

Busshin wa totoshi, Busshin o tanomazu.

Steven Leacock, the Canadian humorist, said it best: "I'm a great believer in luck . . . the harder I *work,* the *luckier* I get!"

Not to step on any religious toes, but no matter how you look at it, we're still pretty much on our own. Even if your particular belief system says *you* have to prostrate *yourself* before *your* respective god . . . *you* still have to make the first move. Even when your P.O.'d deity decides to dump you in the belly of a whale for a few days till *you* see things his (or her) way . . . *you* still have to make the "choice" to see things his or her way.

Likewise, if *your* religion requires *you* to pray in a certain direction several times a day . . . *you* are still the one who has to check the compass and hit the ground in order to give god his (or her) fifty. Maggot!

Hannibal the Conqueror, in his "99 Truths"[45] had a thing or two to say about The Gods:

> The Gods favor those who first favor themselves. Trust in the The Gods . . . but always carry an extra sail.

---

45. For a complete rendering of the whole of Hannibal's "99 Truths," see Lung and Prowant's *Ultimate Mind Control* (Citadel Press, 2011), and Dr. Lung's *Lost Arts of War* (Citadel Press 2012).

Likewise the old Arabic saying, "Trust in Allah, but tie your camel!" And, thus we translate Musashi's fifth "Zen" principle (or . . . warning?) as "Respect the Buddhas and The Gods without counting on their help."

Whether your belief helps you get there or prevents you from getting there, *you* must first choose to believe. And what's that old playground taunt? "Choose right, choose wrong, study long, study wrong!"

Or, as Attila the Hun advised:

> Trouble The Gods little. Neglect them never. Trust them even less!

"The most vital quality a soldier can possess is self-confidence, utter, complete, and bumptious."
—**General George S. Patton, 1944**

II.

Musashi: The Method

"Learn to judge the quality of each thing. Perceive and understand that which is not visible from the outside."
—*Gorin no sho*

MIYAMOTO MUSASHI FUNCTIONED on many levels during his life, not always smoothly progressing from one level to the next sequential level, yet always onward and upward, toward the perfection of self and art.

As with the man, so, too, with his "art," and so, too, our (1) appreciation and (2) application of his philosophy (and perhaps) just a little of his physical prowess.

Thus, Musashi offers himself and his art to us for study on several levels, dependent upon our enthusiasm, attention level, and dedication.

To begin, there is no end to literature about Musashi: from scholarly biographies like Kanji Tokitsu's *Miyamoto Musashi: His Life and Writings*[1] to various incarnations of Musashi appearing—here as rogue, there as rescuer of both damsel and *Daimyo!* in sensationalist and

---

1. Shambhala (2004).

sometimes salacious fiction, to books on how to use the "Musashi Method" to storm Wall Street and take over Tokyo like Godzilla!

Likewise, movies ranging from the fantastic to the factual abound covering the deeds and daring-do (real and imagined) of Japan's *Kensei*. One such series of movies worthy of note is the 1960s five-film set with Yoshikawa Eiji in the starring role in *Miyamoto Musashi* (1961), *Miyamoto Musashi II: Duel at Hannya Hill* (1962), *Miyamoto Musashi III: Birth of the Nito-ryu Style* (1963), *Miyamoto Musashi IV: Duel at Ichiyo-ji Temple* (1964), and *Miyamoto Musashi V: Duel at Ganyu* (1965).[2]

A "purist" would, of course, immediately dismiss such cinematic and fictional flotsam and jetsam in favor of more "scholarly significant" works, but we should not be so quick to do so.

Do you recall our previous discussion (on the *tantric* view of life, or the *Taoist* view, if you prefer), that there isn't any more of the "essence" (*chi*) of the Universe in a temple than there is to be found in a whorehouse—a man (or woman) truly seeking "truth" and "enlightenment" is liable to stumble across the "secret of the Universe" in any place, at any time?

In Hinduism, you'll find temples dedicated to creatures considered vile in the West: the rat and the snake, for instance. Yet, should you take time to inquire, it might be explained to you that, one day, while enraged and heavily armed and barreling down the road intent on murdering his neighbor for some real or imagined slight, a would-be assassin was suddenly startled by a deadly *cobra* slithering across his path!

In an instant, all thought of murdering his neighbor vanished from the man's mind as he was suddenly confronted by his own possible death at the hand (or rather fangs) of the cobra.

And, in that same instant, that man found enlightenment.

Realizing the sanctity of all life, embracing the concept of *Ahimsa*, he not only became a holy man on the spot but, on that same spot, spent the next twenty years of his life building a temple to serpents, for

---

2. Available in DVD format from AnimEigo.

that is the *form* in which God appeared to him, to prevent him from doing his neighbor harm.

Or, how about this: Do you recall the popular 1970s TV series *Kung-fu* starring David Carradine? Even though (at the time) David Carradine (as well as many of those other riddle-spoutin', butt-kickin' "priests" at the Shaolin temple) knew little or no martial arts, still the show inspired millions of would-be Grasshoppers worldwide to (1) take up the practice of martial arts, and (2) try snatching the pebble from anyone's hand who'd stand still long enough! And credit where credit is due: many people got "turned on" to Eastern philosophy in general and Buddhism in particular from watching that show.

So . . . while it would be nice if *everyone* had the mental capacity (and attention span) to learn medieval Japanese and study ancient scrolls on strategy and *kenjutsu,* most of us have neither the patience nor the pocketbook to undertake such a pilgrimage.

But does that mean we can't learn to *appreciate* and even *apply* the "Musashi Method" to our own lives?

Does that mean we can't be "inspired" by his lore and legend, that we can't learn from his example and from the writings he left behind (even if those writings weren't specifically written for us)?

Of course not. A close encounter with a poisonous viper (or, in Jonah's case, a really big fish!) can inspire us to do the Lord's labor, while reruns of *Kung-fu* or *The Wild, Wild, West*[3] might inspire us to study martial arts or even take another stab at understanding Eastern philosophy.

Or, we might be "inspired" to study martial arts after getting mugged at the ATM. (Does God wear a ski mask and sport a Glock?)

Your "inspiration" can come from any of a million faces in any of a million places. Perspiration can only come from *you.*

> While war is terribly destructive, monstrously cruel and
> horrible beyond expression, it nevertheless causes the

---

3. Star Robert Conrad was a devoted and accomplished martial arts enthusiast, and it shows in every one of his fight scenes!

divine spark in man to grow, to kindle, and to burst into a living flame, and enables them to attain heights of devotion to duty, sheer heroism, and sublime unselfishness that in all probability they would never have reached in prosecution of peaceful pursuits. —Major-General John A. Lejeune, *The Reminiscence of a Marine* (1929)

It is the readiness of the mind that is wisdom. —Shunryu Suzuki, *Zen Mind, Beginner's Mind* (1970)

Closely examining Musashi's *Gorin no sho*, we find five basic themes running through his strategy, making up the "Musashi Method."

MUSASHI METHOD #1: BECOME YOUR ENEMY

To "become your enemy" means to imagine yourself in your enemy's position, to say to yourself, "Given his *resources,* taking into account his *past actions*, how would I react/respond if I were in his position?"

This is not as simple as it first sounds. What's that old saying about a skunk not being able to smell his own ass?

It's actually quite difficult to "think" like another person thinks. Our own ego keeps getting in the way, causing us all too often either to underestimate or else overestimate what our enemy is capable of.

Sun Tzu literally wrote *the book* on this, his *Ping-fa, Art of War:* "*Know yourself and know your enemy,* and in a thousand battles you will never be defeated."

Believe this: while you're trying to "get inside your enemy's head," if he's smart, he's trying to do the same to you!

All too often we whitewash over those parts of ourselves—past failures, secret fears, desires—we (1) don't want others to see, and (2) often refuse to admit to ourselves even exist.

As a result, we deceive both others *and ourselves* by painting a grandiose portrait of ourselves and our motives (no matter how distorted, outdated, or falsely hued!), a picture we then proudly display to either attract or else intimidate others.

This is the "mask" we show the world.[4]

Musashi admonishes us: "Don't let the enemy see your spirit." In other words, don't let the enemy know what you're thinking. Don't let him know if, and where, you are weakest, and never let him see your "real face."

In today's parlance, "Never let 'em see you sweat!"

Like the narrator hero of Edgar Allan Poe's highly instructional *Cask of the Amontillado* (1846),[5] we must sometimes endure "a thousand insults," biting our tongue, honing our blade in the silent dark, while keeping our true intent disguised behind a ready smile until the day of rising and retribution finally arrives. Other times, we may be called upon to play the crippled jester, like young Claudius,[6] so as to make our enemy think we pose no threat to his throne.

Ah! But is your enemy thinking the same thing?

Our enemy, too, hides his "spirit," his skullduggery, his attack plans. His "true face" he keeps hidden behind that garishly painted, distracting face and facade he displays and plays to the world. Like Hamlet's women, God gave him one face, but he paints for himself another!

In order to defeat him, we must get a peek behind that mask, in order to "discern his spirit" as Musashi instructs, thus we "discover his resources." From there, Musashi promises, "It is easy to defeat him with a different method once you see his resources."

"To become the enemy" means to think yourself into the enemy's position. In the world people tend to think of a robber trapped in a house as a fortified enemy. However, if we think of "becoming the enemy" we feel that the whole world is

---

4. See also "The Masks We Wear" in Lung and Prowant's *Mental Dominance: The Art of Ninja Mind Power* (Citadel Press, 2009).

5. Teaching patience, and giving us the "rules" for revenge.

6. Roman emperor 41–54 A.D.

against us and there is no escape. He who is shut inside is a
pheasant. He who enters to arrest is a hawk. You must
appreciate this.

—*Gorin no sho*[7]

MUSASHI METHOD #2: UPSET YOUR ENEMY'S BALANCE

As discussed in the section on "*Senki*: Developing Your War-Spirit," distracting, confusing, and otherwise dis-spiriting your opponent all fall under the heading of "unbalancing" him, making him unsure of his "footing"—both physically and *emotionally*. Thus Musashi tells us: "Victory is certain when the enemy is caught up in a rhythm which confuses his spirit."

At the top of Musashi's list of ways to "unbalance" a foe are Danger, Hardship, and Surprises—all designed to induce what Musashi refers to as "fluctuation of the enemy's spirit." Think of this as introducing a virus into his computer, a "glitch," causing him to hesitate, second-guess himself, with the goal of preventing him from (1) seizing the initiative, right, *sen*, and (2) following through with his battle plan.

The *Gorin no sho* tells us that, having succeeded in unbalancing our opponent, we can then "win by attacking the enemy when his spirit is warped." Musashi explains this by pointing out how we can unbalance an opponent during one-on-one combat by disconcerting him (1) with our sword (naturally!), but also (2) with our body language ("attitude"), and (3) with only the power of our voice.[8] It's not hard to see how these three—sword, body, and voice—can likewise be applied to psychological combat as well: we can use deliberate *body language* to confuse, irritate, anger, intimidate, and seduce.[9]

---

7. Victor Harris translation, 1984.

8. More of this in the section on "*Shinjiraren*: The Skill of Confusing the Skull."

9. For a complete training course in both spotting and sporting body language for fun and profit (not to mention personal protection!), see the "Body Language" section in Lung and Prowant's *Mental Dominance: The Art of Ninja Mind Power* (Citadel Press, 2009).

The right word dropped in the wrong ear at just the right time (and every combination thereof!) can accomplish as much if not more than poison dropped in the ear of the king of Denmark.[10]

As for the *physical* threat of "the sword" . . . well, as the White House is fond of threatening, "We have not ruled out a *military option.*"

For us, this is where we resort to "The Killer B's":

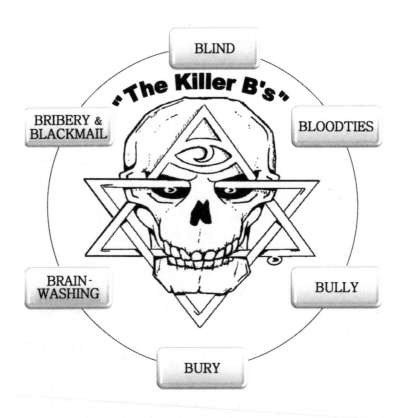

----

10. For a complete course on mastering the words that master others, see "Shadow-Talkers/Return of the Word Wizards" in Dr. Lung's *Mind Control: The Ancient Art of Psychological Warfare* (Citadel Press, 2006).

The Killer B's

The Killer B's consist of six tried-'n'-true methods for "moving" the minds (and the fat asses!) of those people in your life who don't necessarily see things *your* way.

Blind. We keep information from others, information they don't need to know (because then they would move to stifle our plans), or else we don't want them to know (in order to stifle their plans and get to the feeding trough before them!).

Blood ties. These are those real and imagined connections and kinships we use to insinuate ourselves closer to our target. "Blood ties," as the name implies, are usually formed through an actual spilling of blood, for example, having to "make your bones" (i.e., kill someone) as part of your initiation into a violent gang. Blood ties thus often serve as an unseen *threat*, i.e., "I know you killed so-and-so, and if you ever rat me out I'll rat *you* out, too!"[11]

Blood ties can also be information you dig up about another person that you then use as leverage to get them to work for your agenda. More on this when we get to "Bribery and Blackmail."

Bully. The "stick" part of the "carrot and the stick" never gets old. Throwing your own weight around, literally and figuratively, is a good way to (1) unbalance others, and (2) keep them paralyzed through intimidation.[12]

Bury. Literally, you do a Tony Soprano. Figuratively, you "bury" your opponent under a god-awful steaming pile of BS (what Spook-speak calls "disinformation") so that he becomes incapable of functioning, let alone interfering with your plans.

Brainwashing. This entails (1) making him doubt what he already believes, before then (2) making him believe wholeheartedly in *your* agenda.

---

11. Yeah, like I really want to join a gang based on the fear of the mutual "ratting-out" of each other!

12. For a complete course on "Bully Kung-Fu," see *Mind Fist* by Dr. Haha Lung (Citadel Press, 2008).

Far from requiring some exotic *Manchurian Candidate* backdrop, "brainwashing" goes on every day, all around you: Governments do it (a combination of pulling patriotic heartstrings while inducing just the right amount of collective paranoia). Cults do it (instilling an "us versus them" mind-set where nobody "understands" you except for the cult—Hurry, drink this Kool-Aid!). Con men and sundry seducers do it.[13]

For a complete course on "How to Tell If You've Been Brainwashed/ How to Prevent Yourself from Being Brainwashed," see Dr. Lung's *Mind Control* (Citadel Press, 2006). And for a revealing look at how much brainwashing techniques have been and continue to be used by various nefarious cadre (even in the assassination of a United States president!), check out "The Black Mist/Oswald and the Sleeping Tigers" in Dr. Lung's *Mind Penetration* (Citadel Press, 2007).

Bribery and Blackmail. These are no strangers to any of us: "Clean up your room and take out the trash, and we'll go get some ice cream." Rewards *are* bribery.

"If you don't go to bed right now, I'll tell your father when he gets home!" All threats *are* a form of blackmail.

Bribery and blackmail are simply the "carrot *and* the stick." In fact, 99.9 percent of all our dealings with our fellow human beings fit into this particular Killer B's category. Think about it: we work, we get paid, otherwise we starve. And even when we do work, we *must* pay taxes, otherwise we go to jail.[14]

Not to strike too much of an obvious *cynical* note, but perhaps you recall our deciding *there's no such thing as altruism?*[15]

"Everybody gets paid. . . ." Bribery by any other name.

Conversely, from that belt in Dad's hand, to Mom "grounding"

---

13. For a complete course on "The Art of Seduction," see Lung and Prowent's *Mental Domination* (Citadel Press, 2009).

14. Never forget, not paying taxes is how they brought down Big Al.

15. You'll spy this declaration hanging over the entranceway to the Black Science Institute . . . right next to "Abandon all hope, ye who enter here!"

you for life for sneaking in past your curfew, to your high school coach making you run extra laps for being a smart-ass, to your marine drill instructor making you "drop and give me fifty, maggot!" to the afore-mentioned arm-and-a-leg you owe the IRS, everybody gets threat-ened, everybody gets blackmailed. And, one way or another, everybody pays. And so, whether we consciously realize it or not, at an early age, *we* learn how to manipulate—right, *bribe and blackmail*—others to get our way.

Remember your snotty little sister making you do *her* chores, else she'd tell Mom and Dad about you slipping your "study buddy" up to your room?

And, you'd better believe it, with all of today's surveillance wars out there, whether a handheld digital camera poking out through your nosy neighbor's drapes, or that near-invisible government drone flying silently overhead . . . "They *do* know what you did last summer!"[16]

MUSASHI METHOD #3: ONE EQUALS TEN MILLION

According to the *Gorin no sho,* "The spirit of defeating a single man is the same for defeating ten million men."

In penning this, Musashi was in accord with master strategists like Sun Tzu and The T'si Kung.[17]

Musashi's fellow Japanese Samurai strategists also realized this "as above, so below" correlation:

> Winning a battle by commanding a great army should be no different from winning a sword fight in one-on-one combat. —Yagu Munenori (1529–1646)

---

16. For a complete training course on both avoiding *and* ruthlessly wielding "The Killer B's" for protection *and* profit, see Dr. Lung's *Mind Control: The Ancient Art of Psychological War-fare* (Citadel Press, 2006).

17. For the complete history and strategies of the Chinese master strategist known as *The T'si Kung*, see "The Six Secrets of T'ai Kung-Fu" in Lung and Prowant's *Mind Assassins.*

This is an ancient concept: the idea that by studying some part of a thing, we can then extrapolate out to discern a larger pattern.

In Japan the saying goes, "The little *do* leads to realization of the bigger *Do*."

"*Do*" means "way," sometimes used as a synonym to *michi* ("path"). The gist of this concept is that through comprehending the true essence of any **one thing,** we will then comprehend the essence of **all things.** Thus, through diligent **practice** of a martial *do,* for example *kendo* or *judo,* we may discover the "meaning" of the Universe-at-Large.

This concept is based on the Taoist belief that everything in the Universe is made up of a singular essence: *Chi* is everywhere, always, and perfect. Therefore there is not a little more *Chi* in a temple, a little less *Chi* in a whorehouse. It stands to reason then that by studying a single grain of sand, we would in effect be studying the entire Universe.

A more down-to-earth application: do we not sometimes judge a person by a singular act or a singular lapse in judgment, a singular shirking of one's duty?

The Western skill of reading "body language" in general, and the Chinese art of face-reading[18] in particular, "judge" the whole of a person by specific, observable, body cues.[19]

Likewise, psychoanalysts listen for "Freudian slips" in their patients' dialogue, verbal *faux pas* that give revealing insight into the true mind-set of the person on the couch.

Whether a swordfight on the battlefield, a corporate contest of egos in the board room, or a little seduction primping and pandering verbal prelim before the tangling of limbs in the bedroom, your notic-

---

18. For a complete course on *Siang-Mien,* the art of Chinese face-reading, see "Getting Some Chinese Face" in Lung and Prowant's *Mental Dominance: The Art of Ninja Mind Power* (Citadel Press, 2009).

19. For a complete course on body language, see "Shadow Walkers" in Dr. Lung's *Mind Control* (Citadel Press, 2006).

ing minute fluctuations and flaws in others' speech and actions can be the key to your finding that chink in your opponent's physical or psychological armor.

The most worthy of warriors, the grandest of kings, can all too easily be brought low by the smallest *unguarded* emotion.

Says Attila:

> My enemy's anger only dulls his argument, while it sharpens my sword!

Once Musashi had successfully bested a student from a particular school, he had no problem (nor the desire!) with fighting other students, even the "Master" of that particular school—since they were all bound to fight the same way.

It stands to reason that, if he could discern the particular *individual* style an opposing general favored, that general would, either consciously or subconsciously, bring that same mind-set and set of moves to the battlefield when commanding ten million men.

Human beings, being creatures of habit, tend to stick with what works, at least until it no longer works (and sometimes even beyond then!). Unfortunately, for such "stubborn" and "shortsighted" people, they end up running into a Musashi who *does* (1) imagine other possibilities, and (2) *does* innovate and invent new strategies and tactics when necessary. The latter "Musashis" prosper. The former "stuck-in-the-muds" only end up eating dirt before they're then buried in it!

Conversely, on the more positive side, small successes pave the way for bolder undertakings. Accomplishing sub-goals helps bring our grand goal more clearly into view. The example Kensei Musashi gave for this is the way we can build a large statue of The Buddha from a one-foot-tall model.[20]

---

20. More on this in a minute in the section on "Musashi's Zen."

MUSASHI METHOD #4: TWO SWORDS ARE BETTER THAN ONE

"The reason we have a 'back-up plan' is so we never have to back up!"
—C. B. Black

Musashi was born left-handed. If Musashi's father (and his other teachers?) were anything like many modern parents, they might have encouraged (else *punished!*) young Musashi into using his "normal" right hand. As a result, adult Musashi was ambidextrous—able to wield his sword with equal skill using either hand. From being able to use either hand effectively, to arming yourself with *two* swords being therefore no great leap.

Many schools of *kenjutsu,* then and now, taught students to wield both their long-sword and their shorter sword simultaneously.

Since the buckler and shield as was favored in the West never caught on in Japan, a Samurai's short sword could be used to block, parry, and strike.

Yet even those in awe of Musashi's mastering (and then improving upon) the art of fighting with two full-sized *katana* simultaneously, all too often miss the deeper level of meaning hidden within Musashi's "Two Swords School" (*Nito-ryu*).

Metaphorically, "Two Swords" means:

• Always have a "backup plan," and
• Always bring all your resources to bear.

Musashi urged his students to develop what he called "a twofold gaze of both sight and perception."

According to *Kensei*: "Perception is strong, sight is weak."

What Musashi meant by this is that the physical eye (along with our other senses) can easily deceive us—especially with "help": from our wily foe!

To counter this, we need develop a deeper, more intuitive perception, one that employs the "twin swords" of both *heart (i.e., instinct/intuition)* and *mind (thought and reason).*

Like all Samurai, Musashi embraced *bunbuitchi,* "pen and sword in accord," the ideal of balance sought by all Samurai between the martial arts and the liberal arts.

Recall that during his life, Musashi mastered not just weapons, but the calligrapher's brush and the potter's wheel, as well. This revisits the Taoist concept of "as above, so below," that we may know the whole of the Universe-at-Large if we can but apprehend the true essence of but a single of its far-flung molecules. Thus Musashi instructs us:

> Know the smallest things and the biggest things,
> the shallowest things and the deepest things.

In today's parlance, "the more you know, the better you throw!" In other words, the more (1) access to real-time intelligence and the more (2) experience you have, the more likely you'll be able to turn challenge and change to opportunity and overcoming of your enemies.

On still another level, we can see our "Two Swords" as being the two hemispheres of our brains, each with differing, often opposing preferences. And while each side of our brain has its place and purpose, the more we can integrate the two parts, like two *katana* filling Musashi's fists, so, too, the whole of our integrated mind becomes greater—more deadly—than the sum of its parts.

For example, if we know ourselves to be "concrete" (left-brain dominant), we might want to "balance" ourselves out by taking up more right-brain hobbies, like music, painting, or other arts.

Conversely, a right-brain-dominated person might "stretch" their mind by doing math problems.

Since most left-brain-dominated people are also good listeners, picture puzzles would be a challenge to them.

Of course, once you peg your foe as either right- or left-brain dominant, you can purposely clutter his path with obstacles of the opposite hemisphere. (More on using *and abusing* this right-brain/left-brain connection in the following section on "100 Secrets of the Samurai".)

TRAITS

Left Brain

Verbal, uses words to describe things.

Keeps good track of time.

Analytic, figures problems out step by step and part by part.

Abstract and symbolic uses symbols and word representations easily.

Concrete thinking, relates to things as they are at the present time.

Logical and linear.

Sequential (A-B-C . . . 1-2-3).

Objective.

Catchphrase: Hmmm . . . (pondering).

Mathematical (uses numbers to measure and count his world).

Most left-brain dominant people are listeners.

Right Brain

Nonverbal, uses hands, temporal, draws pictures, and designs in the air when talking.

Nontemporal. No sense of time.

Not good with schedules.

Synthetic, sees the "whole," the big picture just by looking at the parts.

Intuitive, a good guesser!

Makes cognitive leaps.

Subjective.

Catchphrase: Aha! (realization).

Metaphorical (uses images and metaphor and simile to describe his world).

A right-brain-dominant person tends towards being a watcher or toucher.

Key: Listen for his use of words and phrases indicating his watcher-listener-toucher orientation.

MUSASHI METHOD #5: NO SWORD IS BETTER THAN TWO SWORDS

Imagine his enemies' surprise when Musashi showed up *sans* sword, instead carrying a wooden sword he'd carved himself, a tree limb, even an empty scabbard.

This was Musashi's "No-Sword" or, if you prefer, his "Mind-Sword."

The Way (*Do*) of Musashi's No-Sword Mind-Sword is to live and breathe *unpredictability*. This fifth Musashi principle can be seen as the culmination of his four previous principles:

- **Become Your Enemy**
- **Upset Your Enemy's Balance**
- **One Equals Ten Million**
- **Two Swords Are Better Than One Sword**

Imagine *the look* on Sasaki Kojiro's face when Musashi showed up for their swordfight carrying a wooden sword he'd whittled from a rowboat oar...No! I mean *really imagine it*. During your Z-E-N meditation technique, *visualize* this look of confusion (and perhaps dread) on your enemy's face. Then, as you confront him, now imagine (superimpose) the look onto his face.

You will be assured of victory when you can successfully cause that same Kijiro look to appear on *your* enemy's face.

> "When you cannot be deceived by men, you will realize the
> wisdom of strategy."
> —Musashi, 1645

III.

Kidoku: The 9 Secrets of the Samurai

> *"Let us not say to ourselves that the best truth always lies in moderation, in the decent average. This would perhaps be so if the majority of man did not think on a much lower plane than is needful."*
> —Maurice Maeterlinck, 1862–1949

THERE IS A WORD in Japanese: *Kidoku,* most often translated as "ability," the skills one possesses. But *Kidoku* also carries within it the nuance of "how" that "ability" is *applied*.

There's a mighty chasm between "grudgingly" doing a task and instead attacking and accomplishing that same task with duty, direction, and determination, with *élan*.

For this reason, the Samurai skills that follow are often referred to as "The 9 *Secret* Ways," even though most of the tactics, techniques, and, yes, *dirty tricks* that make up these nine skills have been known and practiced, in one form or another, with varying degrees of adroitness and accomplishment, for centuries.

The *real* "secret" to these nine skills is not in acquiring the phys-

72

ical and mental skills themselves, but rather in how the diligent pursuit of these skills transforms those skills—further honing and refining those skills for those who come after—and, most importantly, how the acquiring of such skills inevitably *transforms* the students themselves.

Each skill we acquire changes us by opening more doors for more opportunity to present us with more choices.

Always, the entertaining of new and novel ideas floods our brain with new opportunities, new possibilities, new choices, and, yes, new fears as well.

Most people are scared to death of change. Having too many choices frightens them as well.

There are a few who do willingly accept challenge and change and more choice . . . when confronted by them.

Ah, but there are those fewer still who actively seek—nay, *stalk*—challenge and change and constantly demand more choice—more *say*—in their lives.

Be one of those people.

Begin here.

NIN-RIKI: DEVELOPING MIND POWER

"This mental training gave the samurai the edge—and the certainty—they needed to act effectively and decisively in difficult situations. It proved to be an invaluable aid not just in combat, but in their roles as leaders and rulers as well."
—*Boyé Lafayette De Mente, 2005*

Nin-Riki is the mental power that allowed Samurai like Musashi—and that will allow us—to "know" the future.

We will "know" the future not because we were born with ESP, nor because The Gods have seen fit to grant us the blessing (or curse?) of revelation. We will develop this power to see into the future by learning to first *see things as they really are,* before then developing the ability to *see through things,* perceiving intent, thus knowing beforehand what is going to happen by intuitively anticipating others' thoughts and actions.

Techniques successfully employing this *Nin-Riki* power are known in Japan as *atari-kokoro,* and are sometimes referred to as *kiai-shin-jutsu.*

It has oft been said that the average human being uses only 10 percent of their brain. . . .

First, *stop being average!*

Second, the truth is that while all our physical brain is up and running at any given time—even when we sleep—we do only *consciously* use a small percentage of our *mental potential* and, of that "10 percent" we do consciously employ, most of us don't use even it *efficiently.*

Accomplished warriors like Musashi learn early on that *survival begins in the mind,* and that ultimate victory comes about only through mastering the *Atari-shin* . . . the Mind-Strike! The first and final strike is always the Mind-Strike.

Medieval *Shinobi* Ninja faced great physical and mental challenges on a daily basis, not the least of which was the chronic stress of being under constant threat of capture, torture, and summary execution from both their Samurai foes and from rival Ninja.

To combat this stress, Shinobi mastered the art of *seishin-shugi*, literally "mind-over-matter."

It's well-documented how Musashi went out of his way to learn the "Ways" (*do*) of the Ninja, and it doesn't take the stretching of our imaginations to see him studying *seishin-shugi* as well. Those who insist "Musashi the prodigy" had no teachers will, of course, maintain that he, likewise, didn't learn *seishin-shugi* from anyone. Yet none will argue that—however he came by it—Musashi *did,* indeed, possess this Nin-Riki mind power.

Ninja students (and Musashi?) began training by learning the basic traditional and technical aspects of their chosen warrior craft in order to survive.

Dead students don't graduate. Therefore, in order to *master* their craft, the ninja student had to transcend, pass beyond, the mere regurgitation of their lessons, surpassing rote recitation and the mere repetition of physical skills.

Perfection of any "skill" requires perfection of the "skull" as well. At its most basic this means a student clearing their mind of past "Mama, Trauma, and Drama": (1) childhood fears and attachments; (2) trauma, especially that felt in the early years of life, shocks to the system that hack grooves of pessimism, helplessness, and paranoia so deep into an already pliable psyche that no amount of later deprogramming and training is likely to fill in; and (3) the day-to-day grind of human drama, i.e., small-minded dogs barking at one another over ever-smaller pieces of already molding meat!

Ninja *Jonin* recognized that the first step in training students was wiping those students' minds clean of such psychological hindrances and mind filters (e.g., self-doubt, phobias, unresolved conflict, and prejudice), thus freeing up—*unleashing!*—the limitless potential and natural flow of an unclouded mind.

Likewise, we today need to fearlessly uncover our own psychological filters (Mama, Trauma, and Drama!), those mental programming *glitches and viruses* that prevent us from seeing the world clearly.

For survival's sake we must ruthlessly root out these potentially fatal personality faults and mental fissures before our enemies do.

Physical circumstances all too often overpower the *untrained* mind:

> Faced with a threatening challenge or confronted by overwhelming odds, the untrained body panics. It is left to the mind to realistically access the situation and decide the proper course of action: flight or fight, resistance or surrender, life or death. . . . A trained man is an asset, a tool for survival. —Dirk Skinner, *Street Ninja* (1995)

In the face of unexpected—let alone *overwhelming*—force and impossible odds, it's natural that confusion, doubt, and fear seep in and creep in, causing us to falter and fall. Dr. Lung repeating himself again: *Doubt is the beginning of defeat.* Yet, to a determined mind, doubt can also be the first step on the road to discovery.

Doubts and fears are dust[1] and stains on the mirror of our mind, a mirror that should, ideally, perfectly reflect both our real self as well as the reality of the world around us. Instead, all too often our dirty mirror reflects only halfheartedly, imperfectly, because of the "dusts" of past disappointment, present disturbance and depression, and future dread.

Calculated on incorrect and imprecise information, an enterprise is doomed to fail.

In order to remain in a constant state of readiness to do battle, be that battle physical or a no-less-lethal mental challenge, we must follow the lead of men like Musashi and cultivate *makoto,* the "stainless mind."

Makoto, a term borrowed from Zen Buddhism, promotes a balanced state of mind allowing us to remain calm even when staring into the face of the most trying of circumstances.

Developing *makoto* requires we actively cultivate two skills:

- *Haragei* (awareness), and
- *Rinkioken* (adaptability).

Cultivating Awareness

Mastering *makoto* first requires we master the full use of our five senses. The sharper our five senses, the keener the edge of our Mind Sword!

When we're children we naturally use all of our senses to explore the world around us. But as we grow older, our senses begin to dull

---

1. See "The Six Dusts" in Dr. Lung's *Mind Control: The Ancient Art of Psychological Warfare* (Citadel Press, 2006).

until, by the time we reach adulthood, our senses are not as balanced and we tend to favor one, or at the most two, senses over the rest.

For example, according to the science of Neurolinguistic Programming (NLP for short), we all function primarily in one of three "sensory modalities":

> *Visually-oriented people*: Processing the world primarily through our eyes, judging by appearances, expressing ourselves in words and phrases loaded with "seeing" references.[2]
>
> *Auditory-oriented people*: People who process the world around them with special attention to sounds and words.
>
> *Kinesthetic-oriented people*: More attuned to "feelings," like to make physical contact with the world around them.[3]

Accomplished warriors like Musashi practiced the full use of their five senses to the point where they would notice every drop of sweat on an opponent's brow, each flick of his tongue across his dry lips, every nervous shift in his weight. They could also "hear" his fear: the hesitation in his voice, that Freudian slip, the nervous clearing of his throat. And they could "feel" his trembling as they shook his hand or else when they "accidentally" bumped into him.

The most accomplished of warriors even claimed to be able to "smell" fear on an opponent. Once dismissed as bragging, science has now proved humans (like other animals) give off various *pheromones*— some designed to attract mates, others that inadvertently attract *predators*!

Used in concert, to their fullest, our five known senses become greater than the sum of their parts, merging to create a "sixth" extrasensory type of awareness that The Black Science Institute has dubbed "ASP" (*Additional* Sensory Perception).

---

2. See "Sensory Modes" in Dr. Lung's *Mind Penetration: The Ancient Art of Mental Mastery* (Citadel Press, 2007).

3. See "More NLP = More TLC!" in Lung and Prowant's *Mental Dominance: The Art of Ninja Mind Power* (Citadel Press, 2009).

This is what the Japanese call *haragei*.

Age permits us to pick up on all those subtle signals others give off *subconsciously*, betraying their hidden emotions of doubt and fear, even lust. Poker players call these signals "tells," because each one "tells" you something about the player sitting across from you.

While financially costly for a gambler, giving off a "tell" you're unaware of, but one your enemy picks up on, can literally cost you your head on the battlefield!

"Tells" include minute fluctuations in body language (licking your lips in anticipation when you get a good poker hand, crossing your hands and legs when feeling defensive, etc.), and those fleeting facial "tics" (called *micro-expressions*) that flash to an observant interrogator that you're lying your ass off.

The effect of using their five trained senses together, having merged them into that ASP "sixth sense," gave the impression to the indolent and uninitiated that Masters of the Mind Sword like Musashi possessed ESP, even magical powers.

Surely you can see the advantage in allowing—encouraging—your enemies into believing you possess "magical powers" of the mind?

Ninja, as well as other shadowy cadre down through the ages, deliberately directed the *disinformation* toward their enemies that they, indeed, possessed both "occult" origins and "supernatural powers."

The Thuggee ("Thugs") cult of India liked people to believe they were actual tigers transformed to resemble men by their bloodthirsty Goddess *Kali*.[4]

Likewise the *Lin Kuei* of China (forerunners of the Japanese Ninja) spread propaganda that they were, as their name implies, "Forest Demons."[5]

The Ninja themselves vigorously promoted the myth they were

---

4. For a complete course on the history and killing methods of the Cult of Kali, see *The Ancient Art of Strangulation* by Dr. Haha Lung (Paladin Press, 1995).

5. See Dr. Lung's *Knights of Darkness: Secrets of the World's Deadliest Night-Fighters* (Paladin Press, 1998), and *Knights of Darkness* (Citadel Press, 2004).

descended from half-man/half-bird creatures called *Tengu* (and on occasion *Oni* ogres).[6]

Ninja also spread rumors often augmented by elaborate *physical* SFX designed to "prove" they possessed *tsuriki fushigi*, literally "supernatural powers." Note the *riki* in *tsuriki* is the same as the *riki* in *Nin-Riki*. "Tsuriki" originated as a Buddhist term meaning "power that is both subtle and mysterious," whereas "fushigi" implies "something that is beyond human understanding."

Again, having your enemies think you possess *tsuriki fushigi* can't be a bad thing.

Nin-Riki mind power goes far beyond *zae,* the intellect of a well-trained brain.

Beyond the physical functioning of the brain, *Nin-Riki* involves the more subtle, harder to pin down processes we call the "mind" (shin). In fact, when trying to understand *Nin-Riki,* the first Japanese term *kokoro* may help.

Kokoro means *both* "mind" *and* "heart," coming closer to the English words *intuitive* and *instinct*. This reflects that, once we master *Nin-Riki*, we begin to hear "whispers" within ourselves—some people call these "hunches" or "intuitions," vague *feelings* that "something just isn't right"; "I need to take the *next* flight instead"; "I'd better look in the backseat before I get in the car."

Once you start paying attention to these "whispers" and, as a result, start *benefiting* from following your "hunches" and your "inner voice," you might be tempted to start thinking you actually possess "ESP"! Don't. What you're "feeling" is the *natural outgrowth* of your paying better attention. And, yeah, since most people go around *not* paying attention, anyone—like Musashi, like *you*!—who *does* pay a little more attention to life will start to look like (1) a friggin' genius and (2) like they possess ESP!

And if human beings do possess some sort of latent "sixth sense of

---

6. For a complete history and training course in *Ninjutsu* (the art of the Ninja), see *The Nine Halls of Death* by Dr. Haha Lung and Eric Tucker (Citadel Press, 2007).

ESP," what better way to develop it than by disciplining and making full use of your first five? Thus Musashi's command to us:

> Develop intuitive judgment and understanding for all things. Perceive these things that cannot be seen. Pay attention even to trifles!

Practicing Adaptability

The *Bushido* code of the Samurai dictated chivalry in civilian life and outlined restrictive rules when it came to acts such as personal combat between equals (something Musashi was infamous for!) and acts of vendetta (*kataki uchi*), like "The 47 Ronin" in 1702.

But if medieval *Ninja* had held themselves to the same restrictive code (something Samurai themselves often had difficulty adhering to!), then there's a pretty good chance Ninja wouldn't have *survived* long enough for us to ever have heard of them!

The greatest of Shinobi Ninja "secrets" was *rinkicken*—adapt or die!

Like warriors in all times and climes (those who survived, that is!), Shinobi Ninja were trained to think on their feet, to improvise rather than adhere to any *rigid* game plan.

Likewise, Ninja *sennin* (Mind Masters) trained to think in unconventional, non-linear fashion.[7] These *sennin* were able to enter—at will—a heightened state of calm awareness that allowed them to function at their peak physical and mental performance. This level of awareness, employing the full use of all "six" senses, known in the West as *"entering the Zen Zone,"* is called *muto* in Japan.

Translated into English, *muto* means "no mind," meaning the ability to take action *sans* interfering extraneous thinking or paralyzing anxiety that causes hesitation.

The Zen Zone is that level of functioning where "stainless mental

---

7. More on this in the *"Sinjiraren: The Skill of Confusing the Skull"* section that follows.

awareness" *makoto* merges with our peripheral physical awareness allowing us to instantly and effortlessly adapt to rapidly shifting circumstances.

Your peripheral body awareness extends out from you for an average of three feet in all directions, forming a circle (*shuhari*) that allows you to "sense" when someone is approaching you. Some detractors minimize this "sense" by maintaining we subconsciously pick up on the approaching person's sounds, smell, even their body heat before we consciously register their presence.

Sennin and others in the East who practice meditation claim to be able to "extend" this "aura" out even further through meditation and other disciplines.

Master warriors like Musashi operated from this Zen Zone, remaining balanced and aware—guarding the walls of their own mind-castles while constantly on the alert for the least sign of weakness in their foe's defensive parameter. (More on this in a minute in the section on "*Senki*: Developing Your War-Spirit.")

Learning to meditate is the first step in learning to enter the Zen Zone at will.

How to Meditate

Meditation is simply the closing off of the *outer* senses in order to better be able to hear the voices of the *inner* senses.

Westerners see the classic "Three Monkeys" of "See no evil, hear no evil, speak no evil" through a Judeo-Christian filter, falsely viewing this ancient Eastern depiction in moral terms. But the original intent for these small statutes was to teach the proper method of meditation: Find a quiet place (when possible), close your eyes and *listen,* first to the minute sounds around you, then to the thoughts that begin bubbling up from within.

Throughout the East, and increasingly in the West, there are hundreds of types of meditation, ranging from sitting in silence to chanting. What all of these methods have in common is that they first *focus the mind* before then *directing* the mind toward specific thoughts and thought-patterns.

Even within specific schools devoted to meditation, the Zen school for instance, we find varying methods of meditation. While there is some debate as to *how much* Musashi himself was influenced by Zen Buddhism, no one disputes that, being the thorough student he was throughout his life, Musashi *understood* Zen—a boast few people, living or dead, could lay claim to. (More on this in the "Musashi's Zen" section in chapter 1.)

Some schools meditate with eyes closed, others use visual aids (Skt. *yantra,* other times called *mandala*) like this.

Study this image for a few minutes. . . . Now close your eyes. Notice how the "afterimage" of this *yantra* remains. Concentrating, try to hold this afterimage in your "mind's eye." Eventually this afterimage will fade. When it does fade, open your eyes to concentrate on it for another minute, then close your eyes, again attempting to hold on to the afterimage for as long as possible.

As your powers of concentration increase, you'll find yourself being able to retain this afterimage for longer and longer periods.

A by-product of this meditation/concentration will be an increase in your overall concentration in everyday life. For example, the lights in your apartment suddenly go out—but in your mind's eye, you retain an accurate afterimage of the entire room. You can easily see how valuable such a skill would be for a warrior like Musashi: Imagine Musashi sitting in a room sipping *sake* when a gang of assailants rushes in. Instantly, Musashi swings his sword, knocking over the lamp, plunging the room into darkness and his would-be assassins into confusion. Retaining the afterimage of the room in his mind's eye, Musashi kills several of his now-blinded attackers before escaping the death-trap.

Musashi would be aided in his escape by his remarkably *focused* hearing, another by-product of meditation.

A perfect meditation for increasing your power of hearing is "The Farthest Away Sound" meditation: Placing yourself in a comfortable position, close your eyes and *listen*. First, notice the sounds nearest you; the ticking of a clock in the room, sounds just outside the window, a bird chirping, perhaps a passing auto.

Now gently "push" your attention further out. Now you hear the airplane passing far above you, perhaps you hear a gathering storm far in the distance.

Some master meditators claim to be able to hear the "singing" of the planets. Perhaps . . .

Would you settle for hearing that burglar hiding in the bushes outside your window? Or perhaps the odd inflection in a disgruntled, recently fired coworker as he's reaching his hand inside that suspicious duffel bag he's brought with him when demanding his job back. . . .

While practicing either or both of these concentration exercises, you can better calm yourself using "Z-E-N Breathing":

Comfortably seated, or else lying down, breathe in a slow, deep breath while mentally intoning "E" (for "exhale").

Having completely cleared your lungs with a full exhale, draw in a second breath intoning "N" ("in," but also a "Z" turned on its side).

Finally, exhale another full exhale while mentally marking the number "1."

Repeat this breathing exercise for as long as practical. At the end of each cycle count "1," then "2," "3," and "4." Having completed 1, 2, 3, and 4, start over again at "1."

This breathing exercise can be used in conjunction with both your *yantra* and "Farthest Away Sound" concentration exercises.

The Ten Minds

There's an old saying, "Be careful what you wish for," and this holds true for meditators, especially beginners.

In the same way first-year medical students often imagine they have every symptom of every disease in their medical texts, so, too, beginning meditators, especially those bringing an inordinate amount of "Mama, Trauma, and Drama" with them into their meditation sessions, often find "bothersome and troubling" thoughts "bubbling" up during their meditation.

Relax . . . It's *not* Satan. Human beings spend so much of their average day running here and there that, all too often, they don't take time to think about (1) the things that really matter, and (2) the things just beneath the surface that are really bothering them. (Yes, it *is* kinda like psychoanalysis, except you're not paying $150.00 an hour!)

Relax, the best mind-expanding mushrooms grow out of manure.

According to the Japanese Shingon[8] Buddhist Master Kukai (aka

---

8. *"Esoteric"* branch of Buddhism, big on the use of *mandala* meditation.

Kobo Daishi, 774–835 A.D.), there are ten "levels" (or types, if you will) to the human mind. Keep in mind (heh-heh-heh) this realization came about 1,000 years before Sigmund Freud lit his first cigar! What Kukai discovered (or at least *perfected* from his studies in China) were the ten levels of understanding and awareness (Jp. *Jujushin*) at which all human beings function.

Shingon Buddhist meditators see each of these "ten minds" as another stepping-stone toward enlightenment. First we "own" them, then we transcend them. But we must never remain contentedly *trapped* within them.

Studying these ten minds allows us to realistically assess our "level of functioning," i.e., how we see the world: for example, through "Goat's Mind," a life dominated by lusts; or else further up this mental totem pole we might manifest "Child's Mind" by becoming religious, albeit dogmatically so. At the pinnacle, we reach a state of "enlightenment," passing beyond selfish concerns to embrace a balanced, non-attached mind—a mind not easily swayed by the doubts, deceptions, and dreads of "Mama, Trauma, and Drama."

Buddhist Masters warn that each of these *jujushin* contain the "seeds" of the other.

Just because we "raise" our thinking to a "higher" level doesn't mean that those "lower" levels of thought (and action) are not still there, ready and eager to re-embrace us should our attention to detail falter the least bit.

Having realistically exorcised his own mental demons (doubts, fears, ambitions, etc.), realistically assessing his own mind-set within the *jujushin*, Musashi was then free to "size up" his opponents, instantly recognizing through their words and actions, or lack thereof, exactly which of the *jujushin* dominated them.

Having ascertained which *jujushin* mind-frame his opponent was "coming from," Musashi was then free to craft a strategy specifically designed to undermine his opponent—readying the sheep for the slaughter.

Adept people-readers (like Musashi) purposely shepherd their opponents to function at the simplest and easily manipulated level of the *jujushin* possible.

For example, for the opponent dominated by an "Unborn Mind," we might play on his superstitious nature—convincing him Lady Luck has abandoned him and thus he should, likewise, abandon his present course of action.

The ability to recognize which of the Ten Minds our opponent is operating from likewise helps us devise *jujushin*-based strategies tailored to that opponent.

There's nothing inherently "Eastern" about this approach. Nor is it in any way mysterious. We all already do this every day.

You talk "differently" to a prospective employer than you do to your buds at the bowling alley, right?

You frame an explanation you're giving to another adult differently than you do when explaining the same thing to a child.

Likewise, when a *sennin*, or an adroit Master like Musashi, realized they were dealing with a person coming from a different "perspective" (i.e., one of the Ten Minds), they instantly modified their speech, and in some cases their body language, to better communicate with (i.e., accommodate) that person.

Con men, politicians (is that redundant?), and salesmen of all sorts do this very same thing: talking to the person *on their level.*

Whereas we in the West might not be as "organized" when it comes to discerning these Ten Minds, we still take them into account. For example, when talking to a religious-oriented person (*jujushin*: "Child's Mind"), we usually keep our cussing to a minimum. When we're talking to a more cerebral person, a college professor, for example (*jujushin*: "Single-Truth Mind"), we try to take our speech up a notch or two. Likewise, when we run into a selfless person ("No-Self Mind," like Mother Teresa, Gandhi, etc.), we usually speak with a little more "reverence."

In the same way, once we perceive what level of *jujushin* our enemy is operating at, we can craft our approach to him based on the inherent weakness to be found within each of the Ten Minds:

JUJUSHIN: THE TEN MINDS

Level	His Outlook	His Weakness/Your Approach
Goat's mind	Has potential for growth. Literal thinker.	Lusts for food and sex. Has no understanding of cause and effect. Feed his appetites till he chokes.
Fool's mind	Strives to be moral. Fears punishment from man and God. Believes in ritual.	Socially influenced, motivated by fear. Has some understanding of cause and effect. Show him how to clear his conscience.
Child's mind	Religious. Literal-minded.	Seeks approval outside self (gangs, religion, etc.). Give him a uniform and he'll follow you anywhere.
Dead man's mind	Worries about dying. Worries about the future.	Builds "immortality projects"—businesses and broods that will live on beyond him. Show him how to "live forever."
No-karma mind	Understands cause and effect, lawful.	Justice obsessed. Follows the letter of the law and believes in an eye for an eye. Help him indict himself.
Compassion mind	Feels mercy and compassion for others.	Easily trapped with sympathy ploys.
Unborn mind	Believes in fate, God, and luck.	Can be fatalistic. Often not in touch with the real world. Feed his fantasies. Let him win the first few hands.
Single-truth mind	Cerebral.	Can be amoral and believes the end justifies the means. Has feelings of false clarity. Praise his insight.
No-self mind	Sees beyond self, thinks of others first.	Trap him with a "good cause" and with sympathy ploys (see Section III).
Secret mind	Non-attached. Self-sufficient.	Do not approach directly. Use a cutting-at-the-edges ploy (see Section V).

SENKI: DEVELOPING YOUR WAR-SPIRIT

*"Hidden beneath a passion for everything graceful and
refined, there is a strange yearning for the pageant of war and
for the dash of deadly onset."*
—Captain F. Brinkley, 1902

Musashi was one of the original "think outside the box" guys. Few are born with this *skill* and, unfortunately, twice as few take the time to develop said *skill.*

Compounding this perennial lack of imagination and enthusiasm on the part of our fellow humans to better themselves is the fact that, even when effort is made, *appreciation* does not automatically lead to effective *application.*

Look at it this way: you may have a true *appreciation* for Shakespeare's writing and Leonardo da Vinci's art, but that doesn't mean you can *apply* that appreciation and write like ol' Willie or do all that cool art and even cooler inventing like Leo.

Therefore, and at the risk of Dr. Lung repeating himself, while many *appreciate* Musashi, just as many run into a problem of how to practically *apply* the teachings of Japan's greatest swordsman to their everyday, modern, and mundane battles: how to win that "perfect job" you've been stalking or how to lose that stalker ex-girlfriend!

If you learn nothing else from Musashi, you must take to heart his cardinal observation that, whether on the battlefield, in the board room, or even in the bedroom:

All battles are first won in the mind.

Musashi was not the first to proclaim this. Other Eastern Masters from Buddha to Sun Tzu have penned those very words, as have Western Masters of equal regard like Hannibal.

To "first win in the mind" involves going beyond mere "daydreaming" and "wishing." (Although, when correctly channeled through disciplined meditation, daydreaming and wishing—here at

The Black Science Institute, we call that kinda thing *visualization*—has been shown to increase the performance of artists and athletes.) Thoughts lead to deeds. But a certain "spark" is required to galvanize thought into action. In Japan the "connecting tissue" between thought and action is called *Senki,* which Musashi understood as "War-Spirit."

Senki can be broken down into *sen* (literally "taking the iniative") and that favorite of martial artists everywhere: *ki.*

Called *chi* in China and *prana* in India, *ki* (pronounced "key") is both "vital force" and the directing of that vital force.

A word familiar to all martial artists, *kiai* is the forceful expelling of breath and focus often accompanied by a loud yell as you strike. *Ki* is "spirit." Hence, *kiai* is often translated as "spirit shout," meaning to focus your whole spirit (will/determination) into your strike.

Thus, *Senki* breaks down to "taking the initiative" and "spirit/force," and we end up with a meaning in English akin to "focusing your spirit in order to gain the initiative."

Musashi calls this "War-Spirit." "Spirit" here doesn't refer to angels and hobgoblins, but rather to a warrior's focus and determination, the place where thought flows seamlessly into action.

Remember that our physical brain (where thoughts run rampant) is just that: a *physical* organ. Thoughts (impulse commands) from this physical organ travel down our physical nerves to our physical hand, which then, hopefully, follows through with the physical task.

Think of *Senki* as the link between that thought and that action, the will (or "spirit") to carry out the action.

Or you might envision *Senki* being your will and determination flowing unobstructed down the deep grooves you've previously carved in your "muscle memory" through your diligent training.

In the famous Samurai text *Hagakure,* we're told that the Way (path) of the Samurai is simply to choose death. Likewise in his "Answers," Attila the Hun warns that "death is not a threat to the warrior . . . it is a temptation!"

Recall our discussion of the difference between a "natural" *reaction* and a trained *response* when it comes to defending yourself? Well, the same holds true for a myriad of situations, not all immediately deadly.

Musashi didn't "think" about what he was doing during a life-and-death duel. He simply *responded* (not *reacted*) with whatever force was appropriate to end the fight. Remember that, in his quest for excellence, Musashi reached a point where he *chose* to no longer take an opponent's life.

To the novice, Musashi choosing *not* to kill an opponent might look like hesitation. Nothing could be further from the truth.

Consider: A young punk walks up to you and says, "I think I can whip your ass!" Perhaps, in your indignation and anger you decide to make that punk "put up or shut up," stepping off into the alley to teach the young whippersnapper a thing or two . . . proving something to him *and to yourself?*

Now, what if that same punk said the same thing to Chuck Norris? And what if ol' Chuck just laughed it off and walked away? Would we think any less of Chuck? Would it ever cross our mind that some punk could actually kick Chuck Norris's ass? No. We'd all realize just how lucky that punk was!

You and I? We might feel we *have to* take that punk out into the alley and take him down a peg or two. Why? Have we got something to prove to our friends? To the other drunks in the bar? Or to ourselves?

Doubt starts fights. *Certainty* ends them, often before they ever begin.

Musashi one day reached a point where he no longer *needed* to kill his opponents. This probably had more to do with the *physical* perfection of his swordplay than it did him suddenly growing what we today refer to as a "conscience," or his suddenly feeling the need to show "mercy."

Physically, by this time Musashi's skill with a sword had reached the point where he could demonstrate his control of a *katana* by cutting in two a single grain of rice sitting atop a boy's head!

As for "growing a conscience," Musashi's times differed dramatically from our own. In addition, Musashi was *Samurai*, and as such, our modern political correctness does not apply to him.

It is the greatest of hubris on our part to judge past generations by our own—constantly changing—concepts of culture and conscience and the political correctness *du jour*.

That each man fits his time is not to a man's disrepute, no matter how disreputable the times he lives in. That a man places family and friends first, that he keeps his word, that he allows no debt to go unpaid, no trespass unchallenged, this is both the making of the man and the mark of the man.

Musashi's *Senki* included:

1. **Focus:** Where we look.
2. **Concentration:** How (i.e., in what manner) we look.
3. **Determination:** What we're looking for.

Thus, whatever the task at hand, we must focus on it with the same intensity as you would if facing a life-or-death situation. So on the battlefield, so in the board room, so in the bedroom.

First and foremost this means:

1. *Getting* your opponent off balance.
2. *Keeping* your opponent off balance.

Getting your opponent off balance and keeping him there applies whether your opponent is a rival general facing you across a battlefield, a corporate lawyer trying to stare you down over a board room negotiation table, or else that fine filly eyeing you from across the dance floor.

Five Ways to Unbalance Your Enemy

Your enemy comes to the battlefield with a plan. You need to *unbalance* his plan.

In martial arts—shy of knocking your opponent out—nothing is more important than maintaining your balance while unsettling your enemy's balance.

"Balance" refers not only to your *physical* balance but to your *mental* equilibrium as well. (This is why we call a mentally disturbed person "unbalanced.")

But before you can unbalance your opponent, you must first learn to understand his inner nature: What drives him? Not only the "mask" he projects to the world, but his *"inner nature"*—the inner beast he tries so desperately to keep caged.

Musashi knew this as *Yuki mireba*—to see beyond the superficial to the reality underneath.

"Seeing" into an enemy's mind is then the first step toward seizing the initiative (*sen*) to unbalance that enemy. This gives us what the Duke of Wellington called the "upper hand":

> We must get the upper hand and if we once have that,
> we shall keep it with ease, and shall certainly succeed.[9]

Musashi's *Gorin no sho* is chock full of tactics, techniques, and tricks designed to give you the "upper hand" by unbalancing your opponent—what he referred to as "moving the enemy's spirit." However, five bullet points best sum up "The Musashi Method" for unbalancing an enemy:

- *Attack where his spirit is lax.* In other words, attack where he lacks focus. Exploit any laziness and/or hesitation you see/perceive (right, *Yuku mirebe*) in your enemy. When a proclivity toward inattention and sloth do not already exist, it will be necessary to *create* it within your enemy. One of Musashi's favorite tricks[10] was to fake a yawn, "passing it on," inducing his enemy to likewise yawn. Seeing his enemy begin to yawn, Musashi struck!

9. August 17, 1803, dispatch in India.
10. Tricks well-mastered are called "techniques." Techniques half-learned are merely "tricks."

- **Throw him into chaos and confusion.** Where a condition of chaos and confusion does not already exist in your enemy and in your enemy's camp, it is necessary to create it.

  Opportunistic con men and politicians (Dr. Lung being redundant again!) purposely *create* chaos and confusion in order to step in to "take command," creating artificial crisis that only *they* seem capable of resolving. At The Black Science Institute, they teach a class or two on this "C.H.A.O.S. Theory," i.e., "Create Hazards And Offer Solutions." *Your* solutions, of course.

  And, of course, where Hurdles, Hazards, Hardships, Hell-on-Earth, and other H-bombs occur naturally, feel free to take advantage of them. Just because someone else creates the crisis doesn't mean *you* can't take advantage. Where one man sees panic, another sees profit.

- **Frustrate and anger him.** Where there's no preexisting condition of frustration and anger, it will be necessary to create it.

  Anger is a most worthwhile and useful emotion . . . provided *you* are not the one who's angry! Yet, even then, often "righteous anger" can galvanize us to tasks we might otherwise hesitate to undertake.

  Anger is the third of the dreaded "5 Warning F.L.A.G.S." (Fear, Lust, Anger, Greed, and Sympathy).

  Even the best of fighters, if they let anger dominate them, are doomed.

- **Terrify him.** Fear is the first of the "5 Warning F.L.A.G.S." Whereas anger may galvanize one to action (albeit often *rash* action), fear does the opposite: paralyzing us into inaction or else causing us to hastily and often hysterically exit-the-stage-left when we ought to stand our ground.

  A little fear in our enemy makes him hesitate. Just enough fear will make him turn tail.

  Keep the ill-winds of doubt and fear forever at your back, never between you and your goal.

- *Take advantage of the enemy's disrupted rhythm.* When your enemy is upset (literally *physically* and *mentally* upset and off balance), thrown "off his game" and "off kilter," he is more vulnerable to both the sword in your hand and to your Mind-Sword.

  In a physical confrontation, we "disrupt" our enemy's "rhythm" (i.e., natural cadence and flow) by moving at odd and unexpected angles, often with what he will initially misjudge as "nonsensical" moves. Remember: Your enemy comes to the party with a plan. You *don't* want to fit in to that plan.

  The same applies when "disrupting" an enemy's mental equilibrium.

This is the basis for all Sun Tzu's art: When the enemy needs you to be near (so his plan will work), appear to be far away. When he needs you to still be far away in order to initiate his plan, don't let him know how close you really are. Simply put: (1) don't play the other guy's game, and (2) don't let the other guy play his own game, either!

Delay, dodge, duck . . . do anything you have to, to disrupt the other guy's plans.

Need we say it? Where such disrupted rhythm does not exist naturally, it will be necessary to create it in him.

What are some tried-'n'-true ways for "disrupting rhythm"?

Musashi used every trick in the book (and a couple he came up with on his own!) to distract his opponents.

There was the aforementioned "passing it on" ploy, where Musashi would yawn, or otherwise allow his shoulders to droop, giving his opponent the impression the Kensei was tired, or else himself distracted. How often have you seen this "passing it on" in action? You look over and see the guy next to you yawning, and suddenly, you feel the urge to yawn yourself. Some scientists now believe this yawning-in-concert phenomenon is a carryover from our less-evolved days when animals showed their teeth to one another to establish dominance. A rival theory is that yawning in response to another person's yawn is a way to establish kinship.

Whatever its origin, Musashi only used "tricks" that worked. (Otherwise we'd be writing books about "the guy who killed what's his name." *What's his name,* in this case, being Musashi!)

Yelling loudly right before you attack, right, a *kiai,* is a time-honored traditional way of temporarily startling an adversary.

Conversely, suddenly lowering your voice while talking will cause your listener to lean forward, often without realizing it. Likewise, saying nonsense words, even unexpectedly saying cuss words, can momentarily confuse an opponent. And "momentarily" is all you need!

Musashi was (in)famous for arriving late to his duels.

Other times he'd arrive early, once even hiding in a tall tree until the opposing party of warriors grew first irritated, then lax. No sooner did Musashi see them relax than he dropped from his hiding place into their startled midst! In their confusion, some died quickly, while others fled in terror. Still other times a challenger would show up ready to test himself against Musashi's sword, only to find himself having to fight a man armed instead with a tree branch, a boat oar, even a lowly fan.

One of Musashi's most effective tactics for unsettling and unbalancing an opponent was simply not to play by the rules—at least "the rules" his opponents expected him to play by.

Against the backdrop of *Bushido,* many Samurai of the time (mostly sore losers) complained that Musashi didn't fight fair, that he snubbed his nose at "tradition," even that he was being sacrilegious, insulting The Code by his "antics."

What many of his detractors didn't realize, some of whom didn't *live* long enough to realize, was that the gist of the Musashi Method could be found in the pages of Sun Tzu's *Art of War.*

For example, rather than wasting time exchanging pleasantries or insults, Musashi would often rush at his opponent without saying a word—startling his opponent with the focus and ferocity of his attack, attacking before his opponent had to "get ready."

This is *pure* Sun Tzu: Arrive at the battlefield *before* your opponent. Attack him *before* he even has time to set up his camp.

All this was evidence of Musashi's overall "War-Spirit": the unexpected unbalancing of his opponent (by hook or by crook!), both his focus and his fury, rushing headlong into battle, *already having defeated his enemy in his mind!*

For example, challenged to a fight with noted swordsman Yoshioka Kenpo, Musashi unexpectedly arrived being carried on a litter, *apparently* near death from a cold. Just as Kenpo and his two seconds relaxed, Musashi leaped from his "death bed" and killed Kenpo with a single blow from a wooden sword. Pulling his two real swords, Musashi then fought off Kenpo's understandably angry seconds!

Sure, hardly sporting by *Bushido* standards but, then again, *Bushido* has been known to "bend" just a little, provided the victors are the ones telling the story:

> Musashi used the power of confusion with deadly efficiency during many of his duels to the death and with hundreds of men he later fought without intending to kill them. It is obvious that individuals who are suddenly confused or thrown off guard are not in full command of their faculties and can make mistakes that they wouldn't ordinarily make. —Boyé Lafayette De Mente, 2005

It's true Musashi often walked a fine line between what was "proper" and "expected" of Samurai deportment and manners.

It is also true he spent most of his life on the road as a *ronin*, not necessarily keeping company with the upper crust of medieval Japanese society. But it was at this "street level" that Musashi learned his best "tricks," tricks that, in his hands, soon became unbeatable "technique."

Even when Musashi overcame a challenger while using some trick he learned from "the other side of the tracks" (think *Ninja!*), those defeated by him could never accept (or admit) they—the invincible *Samurai!*—could be bested by a "ninja" trick. No, that was just

Musashi being Musashi, having bested them or their master by "perfecting" an ancient *Samurai* sword technique, or having developed the technique on his own.

This refusal to accept reality—that Musashi was after anything and everything he could get his hands on to win—and their refusal to accept that some of Musashi's "tricks" might have started out as *Ninja* tricks, gave Musashi an added edge over many of his opponents. Thus Musashi was part master technician, part *trickster*:

> Here to, however, there existed a sharp distinction between the trickster, who (like the *ninja*) was forever inventing new tactics and subterfuges, and the expert, who could display exceptional skill, style, and efficiency, even within the most commonly accepted and strictest rules of his martial specialization. For the latter, it was not so much a question of tricking an opponent with an unknown strategy, that is, taking advantage of his ignorance and, therefore, of his intrinsic weakness (although in many minds foul play was often equated with good strategy). Rather, the expert desired to be genuinely superior to an opponent in those arts in which both were expected to excel. Naturally, those who espoused this mode of behavior were clearly in the minority—as indicated by the abundance of so-called secret ways used to surprise and defeat the unwary. —Ratti and Westbrook (1973)

Clearly, Musashi was *both* Master technician when it came to the sword, as well as Master "trickster" when it came to his unorthodox fighting style ("the style of no style!") and to his adroitness in wielding his Mind-Sword.

No better tale exists of Musashi's *Senki,* of his adroit wielding of his Mind-Sword, than what has gone down in history as his great duel.

How Musashi Broke the Rock

Yamabushi (lit. "mountain warriors") is a generic term used to describe various groups of "monks" who built their monasteries on the sides of difficult-to-access mountains.

In his magnificent *Miamoto Musashi: His Life and Writings*[11] Kenji Tokitsu describes *Yamabushi* as "a synchronistic religion that tends toward mysticism."

Often prominent Samurai—some dispossessed, others merely aged—were "exiled" to these remote sanctuaries. As a result, *Yamabushi* spent more time perfecting their weapons expertise than they did in perfecting their souls.

Down through medieval times, until finally suppressed by Nobunaga and Toyotomi, these monasteries routinely sided with one Samurai faction against another, often even fighting rival *Yamabushi* temples and monasteries.

To the present day, many schools of martial arts (*budo*)—as well as more than one *Ninja* school[12] trace themselves back to these warrior-monks.

During Musashi's time, the *Ganryu* (lit. "School of Rock") traced itself back to just such a habit of monks. This school's founder, Sasaki Kojiro, was renowned for his swordsmanship, so it was perhaps inevitable that, sooner or later, Kojiro and Musashi should cross paths . . . and swords.

This duel took place in 1612, when Musashi was twenty-eight or twenty-nine and was already himself renowned for his mastery of *Nito-ryu,* fighting with two full-sized *katana.*

The two men agreed that, in order to minimize outside interference, the duel would take place on the isolated island of Mukojima.

---

11. Shambhala, 2004.

12. For a complete history and training course in the ancient art of *Ninjutsu*, see *The Nine Halls: Ninja Secrets of Mind Mastery* by Dr. Haha Lung and Eric Tucker (Citadel Press, 2007).

On the day of the duel, fully expecting Musashi to live up to his reputation for deliberate tardiness, Kijiro was surprised to find Musashi already waiting on the island.

Adding to Kijiro's confusion, instead of sporting his two *katana* (as Kirjiro expected), Musashi was armed only with a heavy *wooden* sword he had carved from an oar just that morning.

Further unnerving Kijiro was the fact that Musashi was standing on the beach with the tip of his homemade sword dipped in the sand—preventing Kijiro from judging its full length.

Angered both by Musashi's nonchalance and his obvious dismissal of dueling protocol, Kijiro, perhaps in an act of bravado, threw his scabbard into the water. At which point, Musashi further *unbalanced* Kijiro by observing, "You've already lost, Kijiro. That's why you threw away your scabbard. Because you know, when this day is done, you'll no longer have need of it."

Enraged, Kijiro attacked, his initial strike actually succeeding in cutting through Musashi's headband . . . before Musashi killed him with a single strike to the temple with the wooden sword!

It is said Musashi truly regretted Kijiro's death.[13]

From this tale (oft told, with often shameless, self-serving varia-tion) emerges Musashi's "No-sword" tactic, what today is called the "Mind-Sword" (*Shin-to*):[14] defeating your enemy through the use of strategy (the sword of the mind) versus the sword in your hand. Of course, it never hurts to have a heavy oar handy, as well!

This duel by Musashi when he was in his prime (not that Musashi ever actually *left* his prime!) already shows many of the ploys and prin-ciples an elder Musashi would later include in his *Gorin no sho*:

- Musashi arrived at the battle site well ahead of his opponent (ala Sun Tzu).

---

13. Ibid.
14. Not to be confused with *Shinto*, the native, animistic religion of Japan.

- Musashi was already rested by the time Kijiro came ashore.
- Musashi had already chosen the spot along the beach where the duel would take place. (Though it is not recorded, we can well imagine Musashi may have himself "suggested" the isolated dueling site.)
- Kijiro was flummoxed by seeing Musashi (1) *not* carrying a traditional sword, and (2) by the way Musashi kept the tip of his wooden sword hidden in the sand, preventing Kijiro from correctly judging its length, thus hindering him from judging proper (safe) distance between him and Musashi.
- Finally, Musashi's intentionally cutting jeer, that by throwing away his scabbard Kijiro already knew he was destined to lose, unbalanced Kijiro to the tipping point. Ironic, considering that his initial rush succeeded in getting close enough to cut into Musashi's headband, had Kijiro not allowed himself to become unbalanced, his cut might have been a couple inches closer— killing Musashi!

With this victory, Musashi gives us the best possible example of the *sen* in *Senki*: (1) seizing the initiative, thereby (2) forcing your opponent to fight from a deficit position or, in modern parlance, to "play 'catch-up'."

"Taking the initiative," Musashi *chose* the battlefield, one that would give him a tactical advantage (e.g., by hiding the length of his weapon): he *chose* to use an unusual weapon, a weapon Kijiro had no experience fighting against; and he *chose* exactly the right observation (*taunt!*) designed to bypass his opponent's "higher" reasoning brain, allowing his enraged "lower" lizard brain to take control (actually *lose* control!) and make him act impulsively. Perhaps it was the "higher/reasoning" part of Kijiro's brain that made him throw away his scabbard, realizing subconsciously, as Musashi so succinctly pointed out, that all was already lost.

Before Musashi's wooden sword ever reached him, he had already fallen fatal victim to Musashi's Mind-Sword.

* * *

As already mentioned, the story of Musashi's fight with Kijiro has been analyzed *ad nauseum* by martial arts enthusiasts in general and Musashi fans in particular, told and retold with various intent and invention, abbreviations and embellishments. Notwithstanding, the *lesson* still manages to come through.

Perhaps you recall a similar version of this played out in Bruce Lee's 1973 movie, *Enter the Dragon*, where he tricks the smart-aleck martial artist who's spoiling for a fight to climb into a leaky dinghy, thinking Bruce is about to follow him. Instead, Bruce lets the line out holding the dinghy to the boat, setting the bully adrift behind the boat. Bruce's reply when the bully demanded, "What style do you practice?" was "the style of no style."

Doubt you that Bruce Lee read the *Gorin no sho?*

ATARI-SHIN: MASTERING THE MUSASHI MIND STRIKE

"In his treatise on fighting, Musashi repeatedly said that it was far better to defeat your opponent with your mind than with a weapon—meaning that it was better to first 'strike with the mind to weaken or virtually disarm an opponent' and then, if necessary, use your sword to finish the job."
—Boyé Lafayette De Mente, 2005

In *Kan-Ryu Taijutsu*, martial arts students are taught the difference between a "reaction" and a "response."

We all have *reactions* hard-wired into our DNA: *survival* reactions like instinctively ducking when we hear a loud noise, and other bodily reactions that announce that the body is ready for "flight or fight" (e.g., those butterflies in the stomach, trembling, sweating, dry mouth), all natural biological *reactions* that untrained people mistake for their being "afraid" or even "cowards."

Other "reactions" can be programmed into us through "Mama,

Trauma, and Drama," for example, being frightened by a spider as a child continuing to manifest as arachnophobia in an adult.

Thus, "reactions" are involuntary and often unconscious, and some of them can be learned.

A *response on the other hand is a* consciously acquired, *trained* behavior. For example, say you are attacked by a baseball bat–wielding assailant: as he (or she) swings the bat downward toward your head, catching the movement in your peripheral vision (i.e., "out of the corner of your eye"), *before* the "higher" reasoning and rationalizing part of your brain has a chance to "process" what is happening, the "lower," more "lizard"[15] part of your brain[16] has *already* ordered the body to crouch down (making you a smaller target) and to simultaneously throw your arms up (to protect your upper body from the descending blow).

This is a *natural* reaction and may have saved you from getting injured or even killed on more than one occasion, e.g., remember when that heavy box fell off the top shelf and instinctively—instantly!—you blocked it with your up-flung arms? Sure, your arms got bruises, maybe you even broke your arm—*but you survived.*

While some (primarily sport-oriented) martial arts schools teach students complicated (albeit impressive to the judges!) movements, strikes, and stances, any *reality-based self-defense* school takes advantage of *natural* reactions a student already possesses and then "fine-tunes" those natural reactions into *trained responses*. For example, understanding a student's natural reaction to an overhead attack, a savvy martial arts instructor merely adjusts the students up-flung arms to more of an angle (helping to better deflect an overhead blow rather than taking the full force onto their upraised arms). Likewise, the student's natural reaction of crouching themselves into a smaller target can be turned into a "Chinese Squat" stance (squatting with one leg positioned

---

15. That just means this part of the brain evolved earlier.

16. See "The Beast Within (Who Doesn't Like to Do Without!)" in Lung and Prowant's *Mind Warriors: Strategies for Total Mental Domination* (Citadel Press, 2010).

behind the other), which (1) creates more "spring" in your legs (for counterattacking), and (2) places the legs in position for pivoting and escaping danger.

Tools, Targets, and Techniques

The sequence for mastering *any* martial art is (or at least *should be!*) learning:

1. The Tools,
2. The Targets, and
3. The Techniques.

This holds true whether you're attempting to master a *physical* martial art (e.g., karate, kung-fu) or when attempting to master and wield your "Mind-Sword." All those strategies and tactics that first attack directly into your enemy's mind, ideally paralyzing him from taking physical action.

"Tools" are Musashi's sword, to the *Karataka's* sword-hand "chop."

"Tools" are your weapons: from your "Mind-Sword" to all these weapons, they are merely tools to help you get the job done.

When beginning the study of a martial art, karate for instance, you are first taught "the tools of the trade." These include the various hand positions used for striking and blocking[17] as well as the various ways you can strike with your foot, elbows, and knee, even butting with your head. All these "tools," and dozens of others you'll later learn, are viable striking "tools."

But a hammer is of little use without a nail.

"Targets" are then all the places on the human body that are vulnerable to the striking "tools" you've just learned. These targets are divided into "hard targets" (requiring forceful blows, e.g., the skull

---

17. In *Kan-Ryu Taijutsu,* as in other "reality-oriented" martial arts, there is *no blocking* per se. All "blocks" are delivered with enough force to damage the attacking hand or foot. See Dr. Lung's *Lost Fighting Arts of Vietnam* (Citadel Press, 2006).

and other bones, built-up muscle areas) and "soft targets" (that can be successfully attacked using less-forceful, but no less devastating strikes, e.g., eyes, throat, testicles, knees).

As the lesson progresses, you'll be taught to pair specific tools (striking weapons) with specific targets. For example, whereas a "Spear-hand" stiff-fingered thrust might do minimum damage to the built-up muscles of the abdomen, a Spear-hand strike to the eyes can be crippling. A Spear-hand thrust to the throat can kill. Likewise, a forceful elbow strike to an attacker's abdomen can knock the wind from him, and even produce unconsciousness. The same forceful elbow strike to the temple can kill.

Of course, the best karate strike (tool) doesn't do you a bit of good unless you can get it to your intended target.

This is where techniques come in.

"*Techniques*" are the stances, body shifting, jumps, and rushes that "bridge the gap" between you and your opponent, ending with you in (1) a position where you *can't* be hit, and (2) where you can seize hold of him, sweep his feet out from under him, and strike into your opponent.

For example, a simple arm-lock where you seize the wrist of the attacking arm while simultaneously applying pressure to "lock-out" the elbow with your free hand:[18] this "arm-bar" technique requires you to (1) know the target (elbow), and (2) know the tool (or, in this instance, tools: palm strike, forearm lever, pressing into the elbow with your shoulder, etc.) to use to complete the technique.

Tools, targets, and techniques. The same three apply to wielding your "Mind Sword."

---

18. For a complete course on such self-defense/offensive techniques, see Dr. Lung's *Mind First* (Citadel Press, 2008).

The Lizard versus the Wizard

In Japan "Mind-Sword" is often written as *Atari-kokoro.* At its simplest, *atari* means "to strike," while *kokoro* means both "mind" and "heart" (implying something "deeply felt," a "commitment").

What is the main "tool" of *Atari-kokoro? Your mind.*

To control the mind we begin with the mind. And, yeah, it is kinda like asking the fox to watch the henhouse.

Our *physical* brain, that three pounds of gray goo, *isn't* our "mind."

Our physical brain, that organ in the body, is made up of at least three *warring* parts: our initial "animal brain," directly connected to our spinal column, our "higher" latest-to-evolve pre-frontal cortex that *thinks* it runs the show, and our "mid-brain" mediator that tries its best to sift through a deluge of data sent it at any given moment from the senses via the "lower/animal" brain, along with having to handle constant complaints from the rationalizing and moralizing "higher brain" that we're giving the "lower brain" too much leash!

Back to our trusted example of our mistaking a harmless garden hose for a dangerous snake in the grass:

- Our eyes perceive something lying in the grass next to our feet.
- Our eye (sense) sends this information to the mid-brain or "processing."
- Unable to make an immediate determination of w't it's "seeing" (by way of the eyes), the mid-brain she' off a "stand-by" memo to both the "lizard" in the cel'and the "wizard" living in our pre-frontal attic.

The lizard reacts without hesitation, sends a message ming down the spinal column that says, "Snake! Get us the he'a here!" And *before we can think about it,* we've jumped back si' away from the "snake."

This is a natural survival *reaction* that we literally couldn't live without.

On the negative side, our xenophobic "lower brain" is where all those prejudices (and, yes, *racism*) still reside, all that politically incorrect stuff we'd like to think (that would be the "higher brain" doing that "thinking") we've exorcized from our souls.

Truth be known, a fear of strangers is DNA hard-wired into us. Isn't it smart to be "wary" of someone—a stranger—you don't know?

Better to make a friend *later* than to give a potential enemy the upper hand *immediately.*

This is how our "brain" mechanically operates. So our "mind" is not this physical construct. Rather, think (heh-heh-heh) of the "mind" as the *interaction* between these three parts/functions of the physical brain.

Ergo, if the physical brain is our tool, then the three separate operations of that tool become not only additional tools for us to use (i.e., manipulate), but also the *targets* of our manipulation.

In other words, having gained some semblance of mastery over your own brain, you are now able to wield this brain-tool as your "Mind-Sword."

And since your indolent enemy *hasn't* taken the time and training you have, to develop his "brain" into a "Mind-Sword," your Mind-Sword will now be able to use all the *techniques* you've gleaned from this book (and from the rest of your vast "Dr. Lung Library") to cut through his novice and neglected brain the way a hot knife—or dare we say *Mind-Sword*—can cut through butter!

The various techniques you can use to "attack" into your opponent's mind include those aimed at his "lower brain" (e.g., appeal to his lusts, stimulate his fear response) attacks aimed at confusing his mediator "mid-brain" (e.g., sending him contradictory "misinformation" designed to create confusion and a tug-of-war between his "lower" and "higher" brains), and you can send morally ambiguous messages that cause his higher ever-rationalizing brain to hesitate, slowing his overall response time.

Those ever-trustworthy "5 Weaknesses" (F.L.A.G.S.: Fear, Lust, Anger, Greed, and Sympathy)[19] work perfectly here.

Fear and Lust are the lower brain's bread and butter. It's all pretty much *the four "F's"*[20] with the lower brain: Flight or Fight, Feedin' your Face, and . . . Sex.

When you approach your target/enemy/opponent by distracting him with either something (or someone) he's afraid of, something he's afraid of losing, or something he's afraid of letting happen (especially if he's gonna get blamed for it), and/or with "Honey Pot" (sex) distractions, you're appealing directly to his "lower" (base and *basic!*) urges.

Conversely, you'll have to distract his "higher" reasoning centers with a good reason (or at least a damn good excuse[21]) for why he should do what you want him to do!

This is your classic "Id"[22] versus "Ego"[23] problem that kept Freud awake at night.

SUKI-JITSU: SEEKING THE "UNGUARDED MOMENT"

"The good Fighters of old first put themselves beyond the possibility of defeat, and then waited for an opportunity of defeating the enemy. . . . To secure ourselves against defeat lies in our own hands, but the opportunity of defeating the enemy is provided by the enemy himself."
—*Sun Tzu*[24]

In his (1975) *Zen in the Martial Arts*, author Joe Hyams relates how Bruce Lee taught him it's always better (and actually easier) to improve

---

19. *Gojo-goyoku,* "The 5 Weaknesses," in Japanese.

20. Term coined by author Vance Packard, *The People Shapers* (Little/Brown, 1977).

21. See "Ten Good Excuses . . . but Not One Good Explanation!" in Lung and Prowant's *Mind Warrior* (Citadel Press, 2010).

22. Inborn component of the human personality driven by instinctive (i.e., selfish) urges.

23. Inborn "rational" part of the human personality.

24. 1910 Giles Translation.

yourself than it is trying to make others appear worse (thereby making yourself falsely appear "better" by default).

It's no secret Bruce Lee was a voracious student of all things strategic in general, and an admirer of Musashi and Sun Tzu in particular.

Sun Tzu's adage quoted above[25] breaks down into two distinct tasks:

First, we must make ourselves stronger and more secure, putting ourselves "beyond the possibility of defeat."

Then, we wait and watch for our enemy to drop his guard.

So strongly did Sun Tzu feel about this point—first making ourselves invulnerable, then taking advantage of any lapse we detect in our enemy—that he actually *repeats* this advice later on, in chapter XIII, verse 11:

> The art of war teaches us to rely not on the likelihood of the enemy's not coming, but on our own readiness to receive him; not on the chance of his not attacking, but rather on the fact that we have made our position unassailable.

Musashi, and other Masters of his day like Munenori, translated this *Sonshi*[26] concept as *suki*.

"*Suki*" literally means "an unguarded moment," in other words, any time your enemy isn't paying attention and/or any time you can use distraction to unsettle him.

The skill to recognize (and *create!*) such lapses in your enemy's attention is known as *kuzure o shiru* ("recognizing the instance of collapse"). In one-on-one combat, as in army-to-army conflict, *kuzure o shiru* is the moment when you realize your enemy's resolve is crumbling. Now your enemy might be dense, or stubborn, and either has

---

25 From his *Ping-fa* chapter IV, verses 1 and 2.
26. As they called Sun Tzu.

not yet realized the jig is up, or else refuses to acknowledge his inevitable defeat . . . but *you* do.

In one-on-one combat, Musashi could recognize the least hesitation in his opponent's movements, or perhaps a micro-expression that told Musashi the man's determination had deserted him, that *confusion* now ruled in the place of former confidence.

It was at that moment Musashi struck!

Likewise, in the WWII game of chess between Rommel and Patton, each seemed somehow "attuned" to their counterpart's least hesitation, his least lapse in forward momentum, each eagerly seizing the advantage when this happened. We see this same sort of strategic and tactical tête-à-tête between other equally matched commanders: each jealously guarding their own initiative and inner thoughts, while ruthlessly rooting around for the least clue to what the other guy is thinking.

A more mundane example? Mike Tyson, Buster Douglas. Undefeated Tyson's singular unguarded moment, and we got a new "undisputed Heavyweight Cham-*peen* of the World!"

Kuzure o shiu keeps us alert for the least chink in our enemy's armor—be that chink physical or psychological.

Of course, this is where your *Black Science* shines! This is where you get to use "The 5 Warning F.L.A.G.S.," "The 6 Degrees of Separation," "The 7 Wheels of Power," "The 12 Beasts," along with all the other tactics, techniques, and tricks you've learned at The Black Science Institute to uncover and then exploit your foe's fears, failings, and faux pas.

There are thus two types of *suki*:

- *Natural faults*: Mama, Drama, Trauma. These include inherent faults as well as faults brought about by circumstance. (Right, "Shit Happens!"). And:
- *Created Faults*: Any lapse in your enemy's attention, any undermining of his reputation, any stumbling block of doubt you can

place in the path of that oh-so-sure-footed stride of his (over)confidence, all fit under this category. In Tokitsu (2004), *suki* is defined as a technique used to "provoke" a fault in one's opponent. Right, *Black Science!*

Musashi's Four Rules for Obtaining Victory

"Man does not enter battle to fight, but for victory. He does everything he can to avoid the first and obtain the second."
—Colonel Charles Ardant du Picq, **Battle Studied**, *1880*

Potential weakness is *ako*. Therefore *Eko-jitsui* is the art of discerning weaknesses in your opponent's *physical* defense, e.g., the way he drops his hand after throwing a punch, exposing his jaw to your left-hook.

Eko-shin-jitsu looks for weaknesses in the enemy's mind (*shin*) that can be exploited to confuse, make hesitate, and even paralyze an enemy. Thus we use one or more of "The Five Warning F.L.A.G.S." (Fear, Lust, Anger, Greed, Sympathy) to startle, stifle, and ultimately stop our enemy in his tracks.

Having spotted one (or more) of these five weaknesses dominating his personality, we then employ one or more of techniques of "The Six Killer B's" (Blind; Bribery and Blackmail; Bloodties; Brainwashing; Bullying; and Burying 'Em) to ultimately defeat him.

In the Scroll of Fire, part of his *Gorin no sho*, Musashi gives us "The Four Rules": the victory in individual combat, hence, by extrapolation (since in Musashi math "$1 = 10,000,000$"), "The Four Rules for Winning *Any* Battle":

(1) You must have knowledge concerning your opponent's school. In one-on-one combat this literally means what it says: we need to figure out his style of fighting. Is he a puncher or a kicker? Can we expect a "fair" fight (heh-heh-heh) or is it a down-'n'-dirty, have-your-grandma-slip-you-the-straight-razor, anything-goes street fight?

Even in non-physical confrontations, business for instance, is the man (or woman) sitting across from you at the negotiation table to be trusted to keep their word? This first rule segues into Musashi's second rule:

(2) **Be able to discern your opponent's personality.** Is he trustworthy, or open to deceit? Is he Christian, Muslim, Buddhist? White, Black, Asian? Straight, gay? All these and a thousand other variables affect our dealings with every other human being on the planet. They even created a science for this: it's called *psychology*. Okay, maybe not so much "science" as it is "voodoo," but the stated goal of psychology remains worthwhile: figure out what makes people tick.

What psychology *has* figured out so far (after that whole reading bumps on a person's head thing fell through!) is that a person's personality is both molded and then *re*-molded over and over by Mama, Drama, and Trauma.

We're all pretty much born with pretty much the same basic three pounds of mind stuff. Barring any actual birth defect hampering our brain from operating within "normal" parameters, we still get screwed up by "Mama" (our upbringing, especially in the early years), "Drama" (the social interactions we observe and/or participate in, again, most influential at an early age), and "Trauma" (parental child abuse; being bullied at school; surviving being mugged; going to prison; being dropped "in country" in Vietnam, Iraq, or Afghanistan; 9/11; our swimming through a tsunami; and outrunning three ex-wives!).

Any and all of these—Mama, Drama, Trauma—can scar you for life, at any time in your life. One minute you're livin' high-off-the-hog, next you're homeless.

The important thing is that we *truthfully* examine ourselves and try to work out (or work off) our personality glitches *before* our enemies discover and take advantage of said glitches.

Conversely, part-'n'-parcel of getting the upper hand over your foes is figuring out what "dirty laundry," shame, and shortcomings they're trying so desperately to keep hidden from us.

The closer you get to your enemy's true personality, the closer you get to containing, cajoling, corrupting, and ultimately controlling him. In this way, we ready ourselves for Musashi's final two rules:

(3) Find your opponent's strength . . . and avoid it!

(4) Find your opponent's weakness . . . and exploit it!

Peace is our aim and strength the only way of getting it.
—Winston Churchill

IAIDO: SECRETS OF THE SAMURAI "FAST DRAW"

"The sword drawn—cuts! Hesitation equals death. Having decided on a course of action, act quickly, before your plans are discovered."
—Ssu-Ma, Chinese strategist

Samurai are to Japan what gunslingers are to America's Wild West. Many people are unaware that the classic 1960 Western *The Magnificent Seven*[27] was inspired by an equally classic 1954 Japanese film called *The Seven Samurai*.

Every ten-gallon-hat aficionado knows that any gunslinger worth his salt was required not only to be able to clear leather in the blink of an eye, but also to be able to *instinctively* draw a bead on the third button down on his opponent's vest. "*Instinctively*" being just another name for (1) paying better attention, and (2) training harder than the fellow next to you—the fellow the bear just caught up to.[28]

As with the gunslinger, so with the Samurai.

In Japan they call it *Iaido*—the secret of the fast draw, slipping that three feet of stainless steel from its sharkskin-covered scab-

---

27. And its *less than* magnificent movie sequels and blessedly short-lived TV spinoff?

28. Old hunter's joke: First hunter tells the second hunter, "A grizzly! We gotta outrun him!" "No," clarifies the second hunter. "I just have to outrun *you*!"

bard before your opponent even suspects you've taken hold of your weapon.

Iaido: just one more thing Musashi took time to master.

For Musashi this simply meant getting your weapon to the party before your enemy, what Chinese strategists call *cheng*—direct and to the point, literally.[29] First sword to clear the scabbard won first cut. First cut, best cut—*only* cut!

Iaiso-jutsu is thus the "art of the fast draw" and is divided into four recognizable parts:

1. *Nuki tsuke*: drawing the sword and making your initial strike all in a single movement;
2. *Kiri tsuke*: the "finishing cut"—what Westerners call the "*coup de grace*";
3. *Chiburi*: "cleaning the blade"; and
4. *Noto*: "replacing the blade"—ceasing hostilities, but ready to respond to the next threat.

As with all things Musashi, we can use this *Iaido* outline *beyond* the physical battlefield, employing this succinct method in problem-solving in all our endeavors and challenges.

Nuki Tsuke: Draw and Strike in One Motion!

For Samurai, to draw a sword was to use a sword. Indeed, in polite company, when admiring another's sword, the sword should never be completely pulled from the scabbard.

To continue our Samurai/gunslinger analogy, in the Wild West, to draw your pistol quickly was job one. However, being the first to "clear leather" accomplished little if you couldn't hit the broad side of a barn!

Likewise, to draw a *katana* quickly can be accomplished by any

---

29. Ch. *Cheng*—and *ch'i*, direct force and indirect force, e.g., conventional military forces versus guerilla units.

swift hand. But the *Iaido* ideal requires not only clearing leather but putting your shot—in this case, your blade—where it'll do the most good.

Whether clapping leather or clearing your scabbard, hitting your target with bullet or blade requires either luck or focus. Since the former cannot be trained, it's better to trust your fortune and fate toward developing your ability to focus.

Thus, whether martial artist or portrait artist, focus is ever the key. This tale is told of an elder Pablo Picasso: Having finished his lunch, the always gracious and cavalier Picasso repays the attentiveness of a young waitress by quickly—masterfully—sketching her portrait on a handy napkin. He draws the portrait with but a single flourish of his hand, his pen never leaving the napkin.

"Humph! How long did it take you to draw *that?*" snickered an older, fur-wrapped woman sitting nearby.

"Thirty years, madam. A mere *thirty years!*" Picasso replied calmly—coldly.

So, too, when we watch the master martial artist strike quickly, flawlessly, whether with *katana*-sword or with *karate* sword-hand, we do not see the *decades* he may have had to devote to the practice and perfection of his stance, hand position, his draw-strike and follow-through, and, perhaps most importantly, his *Mind-Sword* focus, all necessary to achieve such a flawless strike. This is *kami waza,* literally "the technique of The Gods," i.e., the perfect stroke.

When the clock strikes high noon, it's a little late for Gary Cooper to start practicing his fast draw.

Once you drop your hand toward your sidearm, the instant your hand grips your sword, the die is cast . . . hopefully not casting *you* in the dying role.

But long before this face-to-face meeting comes the training and the planning, the learning, the preparation—the usual investment of sweat, blood, and tears—your sweat, his blood, the tears of his widow.

This same principle applies whether you're stepping onto the battlefield, into the board room, even into the bedroom.

First: The more you know about the person you're going up against, the sharper your edge. And you can bet whoever you're going up against—rival general, fellow businessman, prospective lover—is going to be trying to find out all they can beforehand about *you.*

All this intelligence-gathering takes place *before* you find yourself standing face-to-face. However, this learning process never ceases. Even when face-to-face, you'll still be "checking out" the other person: noting their body language (relaxed or tense?); the trembling of their hand (licking of lips?); their breathing (even or excited?); their face (pale or flushed?).[30]

But once all this intelligence-gathering is said and done . . . it all comes down to who strikes the first—and final—blow.

Keeping your intentions and your anxieties from your opponent is a given. In Japan this is called "masking your *wa,*" referring to emotional equilibrium, aka your "*wa,*" physically appearing calm even when in emotional turmoil.

Ideally, having mastered meditation and other methods of focus, we actually can remain inwardly calm, even when surrounded by chaos and assailed by the confusion of others.

This is the ideal of the perfect assassin: the man (or woman) who can approach their prey without arousing their would-be victim's suspicion.

This "masking the *wa*" is the ideal whether we're talking one-on-one confrontation (or negotiation) or applying this principle to large-scale battlefield operations.

For Musashi, "*masking wa*" meant giving up nothing to an opponent, keeping them guessing as to his intent right up until the moment it came to draw the sword and cut down the enemy.

---

30. For a complete course on Chinese face-reading, see "*Siang Mien*: Face Reading 101" in Lung and Prowant's *Mental Dominance* (Citadel Press, 2009).

Kiri Tsuke: Follow-Through and Finishing Cut

You might not think a *ronin* rogue like Musashi would have much in common with an accomplished golfer like Chuck Shumway, and yet though separated by 1,500 years and a few thousand miles, next to "Keep your eye on the ball" (or, in Musashi's case, your eye on an opponent's *throat*), both men knew the value of the "follow-through."

All great athletes know the importance of the follow-through, in effect, the importance of finishing what you start with at least as much focus—if not *panache*—as you began your swing.

Ever taken up *judo* or *jujutsu*? The first thing a novice is taught is how to fall correctly. And part of falling correctly includes slapping your hand to the floor (in order to dissipate the impact of being thrown to the ground).

And what was that (in)famous warning whispered into George W. Bush's ear just prior to the invasion of Iraq? "You break it . . . you *buy* it."

In *Iaido*, the first cut generally equals death, but that doesn't mean, having made that initial cut, that Samurai then dropped their guard. A wounded enemy—even a dying enemy—may still have enough life left in him to kill you on his way out the door.

Ever watched a mixed martial arts octagon match? Even when one fighter catches his opponent with what, to the audience, is a surefire knockout, before the already *obviously unconscious* fighter hits the floor, his assailant has probably already "pieced him up," hitting him again and again even as he goes down, perhaps even hitting the now clearly unconscious fighter a few more times before the referee throws himself between them. Does this mean the victor is being needlessly vicious? No. It means the victor is being practical—until he's *certain* (and that means the referee calling the fight over)—the winner doesn't stop hitting someone who might get back up and start hitting *him* again.

To put this "Sons of Brutus" concept into terms Westerners might find more familiar: Don't you just love it when someone pulls off a "fourth down with only seconds left on the clock Hail Mary come from behind" to "win one for the Gipper!" Sure. It's human nature to love those kinds of edge-of-your-seat, come-from-behind photo finishes, especially unexpected wins where the underdog or Cinderella team carries the day.

In Italy they still tell stories about how Spartacus, a lowly slave-gladiator, challenged the might of Rome. In Japan they love to tell stories of heroes like Yoshitsune Minimoto (who, after his clan was decimated, survived and spent years in hiding secretly studying with *Ninja.* learning the forbidden fighting skills that years later allowed him to lead his clan to return and overthrow their enemies); The 47 Ronin, whose tale we've already told; and Ito Ogami, "The Lone Wolf" (who, after his family was massacred, spent years wandering Japan with his infant son in tow, both being hunted by ruthless assassins).

Yoshitsune, The 47 Ronin, and the Lone Wolf all share one thing in common (beyond the fact that all finally got revenge on their enemies), and that is: had their enemies *finished the job,* we would never have heard of any of these heroic comebacks.

History, East and West, is full to overflowing with stalwart spirits of this sort: men (and women) who, though beaten down—some enslaved, some even left for dead—not only survive, but beg, borrow, or steal the will and wherewithal to return to wreak havoc and revenge on those who trespassed against them.

Next to star-crossed lovers, this is the most-prized of *human* stories, with examples found in all cultures.

Machiavelli referred to these as the "Sons of Brutus" (a term first coined by the Romans), meaning simply, realistically, and *ruthlessly*— if you kill the father, you had best follow-through and kill the sons as well, lest twenty years down the road, those sons, now grown, return with a literal vengeance. According to the Romans, by way of Machiavelli, prudence calls for this potentially dangerous element to be completely eliminated. To quote one military genius:

> Strike an enemy once and for all. Let him cease to exist
> as a tribe or he will live to fly at your throat again. —
> Shaka Zulu, 1811[31]

Throughout history, down through to the present day, we've seen the "Sons of Brutus" rise again and again.

For example, in 1995 Serbian forces invaded Bosnia-Herzegovina, reportedly massacring over 8,000 Muslim men and boys in Srebrenica. The world was shocked, that is, except for those few people who actually still study history.

During World War II the fathers and grandfathers of those Bosnians had sided with Hitler, helping the Nazis massacre Serbs. Forty-some odd years later, those Serbian SOBs—"Sons of Brutus" seized the opportunity to take their revenge.

"Following through" applies to all elements (primarily people) left over after an operation (be that "operation" a palace coup or a corporate takeover), elements that could conceivably trouble you at some future date. These "troubling elements" can include displaced and dispossessed refugees, disgruntled ex-employees whom you had to let go because of recent "downsizing," or that psycho ex-lover with a tire-slashing fetish.

To ratchet it down a notch (just in case all this talk of "whacking" the Sons of Brutus before they can come back and whack you is making you just a wee bit uncomfortable), all we're really talking about here is "dotting all the *i*'s and crossing all the *t*'s"—finishing what you start.

To go back to the George-W.-invades-Iraq example: "Shock-'n'-awe" worked wonderfully, but didn't anyone in the White House anticipate all the "policing" and rebuilding that would need to be done following a successful toppling of Sadaam Hussein's regime? This is what's usually referred to as "mopping-up operations" following a victory.

---

31. See *Shaka Zulu* by E. A. Ritter, 1955.

In the board room, this means making sure anyone who might possibly derail your plans is in on those plans—right! Keep your friends close and your enemies closer.

On the battlefield, this means making sure *every single head* of the Hydra is dead and that no soldiers (i.e., Sons of Brutus) are ever going to spring up from the dragon's teeth you've sown.[32]

And, yes, in the bedroom, it means hanging around long enough (or at least *staying awake* long enough) to "cuddle."

Chiburi: Cleaning Your Blade

Having struck the fatal blow, the master Samurai then flicks his blade with such flourish that any blood remaining on the blade is dislodged. An *Iaido* Master always does this before replacing his blade in the scabbard.

This is not only good blade "hygiene," it's also good *mental* hygiene.

"Cleaning your blade," metaphorically, may remind those Westerners (and Easterners, as well) with a Christian bent of the New Testament advice to "shake the dust from your feet" when leaving a town where their ministry has not been welcomed with open arms. Likewise, Easterners (and some knowledgeable Westerners) may be reminded of that similar Buddhist metaphor we've already discussed, of how the mind can be likened to a mirror obscured by dust—symbolic of our ignorance.

In the same way, we, symbolically at least, remove the ignorance (symbolized by dust) obscuring our more perfect self (symbolized by the mirror). So, too, upon completing any task, it's important we discard, leaving behind any recriminations, any "*i*'s" left undotted, "*t*'s" left uncrossed.

In the course of accomplishing our goal, depending on the sever-

---

32. It's called "Greek Mythology," a required course of study at the Black Science Institute. According to Attila the Hun: "Men learned treachery from the Gods."

ity and immediacy of the situation, coupled with our own enthusiasm and ruthlessness, and justifying means to accomplish our goal, there's a likelihood we'll step on a few toes, make a few enemies, unavoidably get a little . . . "dirt" on our hands (or sword blade, as the case may be) along the way.

At the end of any war, having conquered your enemy's lands, you have a choice of repatriating all of your enemy's POWs or else slaughtering them all, potential Sons of Brutus that they are. When you're the winner, the one who'll be writing the history books, you can get away with things like that. In other words, you can be a gracious winner, helping your opponent up after you've beaten him down, or else you can opt for being a complete A-hole, rubbing your victory (among other things) in the loser's face.

Newly crowned "Top Dog," you can start building walls or you can start repairing bridges. You can decide to stand fast with the past or take a chance on the future. The past is usually safer; the future more scary and uncertain. No mystery which one the average person tends to cling to.

Stop being average.[33]

But there are times, even in the heat of battle, during a protracted campaign, during an all-night game of Texas Hold 'Em, when it's time to cut your losses and walk away.

It takes both hands to grab on to the future. So unless you're that four-armed Shiva the Destroyer god of the Hindus, sooner or later you're gonna have to let go of the past.

In the East, Buddhist Masters often compare a man using a rowboat to cross a stream to that of a man seeking enlightenment through the practice of Buddhism. Having used Buddhist teachings to gain enlightenment, having successfully "rowed to the far shore," the Buddhist practitioner is then free to discard the very boat that ferried him to that far shore. Indeed, it would be foolish for him to continue carrying that boat farther than the shoreline itself. In the same way, Bud-

---

33. Reading "Dr. Lung" books is a good place to start. Heh-heh-heh.

dhist practices (meditation, etc.) that help the Buddhist student gain enlightenment can all too easily begin to hold him back if he continues to "cling" to such practices, or if he becomes in any way dogmatic, imagining that the Way that brought him to "enlightenment" is somehow "the only path" to enlightenment.

Noto: Replacing Your Blade

Having accomplished your goal, resist the temptation to rest on your laurels, to pat yourself on the back and go on vacation.

Instead, start *rebuilding* any bridges you burned on your way to the top. Smooth over some of those feathers you've ruffled on your way to becoming cock-of-the-walk.

Be a gracious winner. Or, as Hannibal the Conqueror instructed: "Shame your enemies with your mercy."[34]

Recall what happened to the celebrants of Troy, loudly rejoicing their "victory" over the Greeks with flowing wine and glowing wench . . . even as Ulysses and his comrades used a little horse-sense, and waited silently . . . patiently . . .

After a brief celebration (a way of showing appreciation for those who helped you succeed[35]), call a meeting to debrief your lieutenants, listening to their feedback on how to upgrade performance even more on the *next* project.

If acting alone, *meditate* on actions you could have taken (or anger you could have refrained from) that *next time around* will bring victory to you even more swiftly, even more effortlessly.

Another interpretation of *noto,* as rendered into English, calls for us to literally *replace* our blade, whenever that blade has become untrustworthy (due to wear and tear, etc.).

---

34. Truth XLV. For a complete rendering of "Hannibal's 99 Truths," see Lung and Prowant's *Ultimate Mind Control: Asian Arts of Mental Domination* (Citadel Press, 2011).

35. Take care of your people and your people will take care of you.

Musashi cautioned against favoring one weapon over another, and Gods forbid! against having a favorite weapon.

Even as early as by Musashi's time, let alone *today*, some Samurai swords were highly prized, even to the point of being held in sacred (read: *superstitious*) awe.

Musashi knew that if you favored one weapon or strategy over another, you just made it easier for your enemy to develop a counter-strategy or even craft an actual weapon designed specifically to counter the Samurai sword.

We can further extrapolate Musashi's warning about not favoring one weapon over another, mixing it with *noto*, and take it as a warning about the people around us.

Musashi was a rolling stone most of his life, *adopting* a son only late in life. As such, Musashi had no family or even close friends whom his enemies might target in their hatred toward him.

Today, few of us have the option of becoming unattached, wandering *ronin*. This makes it all the more important that we take better notice, and *a better tally*, of the people in our lives, those who truly benefit us, those who are holding us back, those who might be used against us by a wily foe, and those who could be *turned* against us by an even more savvy enemy.

Some blades *need* replacing. Better your favored blade broken . . . than to find it *buried* in your own throat!

> In Musashi's view there were two facets to victory. First, the opponent or opponents should be killed as quickly and as expeditiously as possible. And second, if any opponents were left alive, their spirit should be totally destroyed so that they would never again present a threat. —Boyé Lafayette De Mente

SHINJIRAREN: THE SKILL OF CONFUSING
THE SKULL

*"Goad your foe into attacking before he is ready, and you will
always gain the advantage over him."*
—*Sword Master Kojiro Okinaga's advice to his young student,
Miyamoto Musashi*

Hiroka Yoda and Matt Alt are spot-on in their colorful and entertaining *Ninja Attack: True Tales of Assassins, Samurai, and Outlaws*,[36] in
which they point out that, while not a Ninja *per se*, Musashi's strategic
use of psychological warfare to disrupt the concentration of his opponents is the stuff of legend.

For example, when fighting a *kusarigama*[37] expert named Shishido,
in order to close with his opponent not becoming ensnared by the
weapon's whirling chain, Musashi first *confused* Shishido by adroitly
twirling his short sword overhead, distracting Shishido, before unexpectedly throwing the short sword into Shishido's chest and then suddenly rushing forward to finish the job with his *katana.*

Confusing an enemy is the first step to conquering him. Doubt
= delay. Delay = hesitation. Hesitation = death.

Whereas the *ideal* of Bushido was two equally matched Samurai
fighting face-to-face, the reality was then, as it is now, as it has always
been: the winners write the history books. Thus, those Samurai who
lived to tell the tale would leave out the part where they'd won more
by the craft of confusion than by a cut from their *katana.*

Of course should a Samurai try such an underhanded ploy and
fail, they would be vilified by the "noble" victor.

And of course, Musashi, while the "Master" when it came to confusing his opponents, was by no stretch of the imagination the only
Samurai who hedged his bets with a little skullduggery and chicanery.

---

36. Kodansha International, 2010.
37. Fighting sickle with weighted chain attached.

The history of Japan in general, and the legends of its various warrior cadre—Samurai, *Ninja, Yamabushi* monks—in particular, is full of the exploits of such tricksters.

For example: trapped on a mountain by his enemies, twelfth-century Japanese Robin Hood Tokakushi Daisuke strapped flaming torches to the horns of a herd of cattle, stampeding them into his Heike enemy, reportedly causing ten thousand of his enemy to fall to their deaths into a narrow canyon.[38]

Another Samurai slathered himself with blood and gore and lay for hours on a pile of battle dead, waiting for his enemy, the victorious Oda Nobunaga, to pass by. His assassination attempt failed, but the memory of his "bold" *Ninja-like* attempt survives.

Still today, when suddenly surprised and outwitted, Japanese exclaim, "*Shinjiraren!*", literally, "It boggles the mind." For their part, Samurai referred to confusing the enemy either into inaction else into making a foolish mistake as *uromekasu*, literally, "troubling" the enemy. Explains Musashi:

> Here is what I call "troubling the enemy": Preventing him from having a confident mind.

Uromekasu is closely related to *kizeme,* a word that refers to the offensive use of one's *ki* (*chi*), *e.g.,* purposely projecting your *ki*[39] "outward" and toward your opponents in such a way as to confuse, paralyze, and/or terrorize them.

Of course, nobody beats the Ninja when it comes to confusing and hoodwinking their enemies.[40]

Down through the ages, Samurai, hero and rogue alike, have also freely used confusion to stifle their foes.

---

38. Hannibal the Conqueror is said to have used a similar ploy to escape the Romans. See Dr. Lung's *Lost Arts of War* (Citadel Press, 2012).

39. Aka Life Force, concentration, attitude and intent, will.

40. For a complete course on the *Ninja* art of hoodwinking, see *Nine Halls of Death* by Dr. Haha Lung and Eric Tucker (Citadel Press, 2007).

No family of respected Samurai were better known for "Dancing with the Long-Nose"[41] as were the Yagu.

Yagu[42] Munenori (1571–1646) was the son of Yagu Muneyoshi (1529–1606) and the father of Yagu Jubei (1607–1650).

Jubei (also known as Yagu Mitsuyoshi), like his father and grandfather before him, was a noted swordsman. He founded the Yagu "New Shadow" school and was a master of the art of *Tsuki-kage* ("Moon Shadow"). In turn, his students were masters of night-fighting by virtue of his teaching them to fight *blindfolded.*

Jubei was felled in battle by a poisoned arrow in 1650.

Jubei's grandfather, Muneyoshi, had also been a respected swordsman and strategist, passing these crafts of skill and skull along to his son, Munenori.

The elder Muneyoshi taught his son well, training Munenori until the boy was both wise and wily enough to know a good thing when he saw it, thinking *and stepping* "outside the box" to learn or otherwise acquire any tactic or technique he could conceivably turn to his advantage by adding it to the already impressive Yagu family arsenal, no matter the origin of said tactic and technique.

Munenori began his strategic studies with his father encouraging him to study under Master Takuan at the *Rinzal* school of Zen, in the hopes of further honing the five samurai virtues: Humility, Loyalty, Courtesy, Wisdom, and Trust.

Kenjitsu-wise, Munenori augmented the fine swordsmanship learned from his father by studying with the *Shinkage-ryu* ("New Shade" school), founded by sixteenth-century Swordmaster Kamiizumi Hidetsume.

---

41. "Long-Nose" being a euphemism for *Ninja*, a reference to Shinobi *Ninja* promoting the superstition that they were descended from the Storm-God Susano by way of his half-man/half-crow *Tengu* stepchildren. Shape-shifters, lone "noses" and long "beaks" being interchangeable.

42. FYI: In Medieval Japan the surname (e.g. family, clan) was always listed before a person's personal name, hence the *Yagu* family.

The *Shinkage-ryu* taught sword fighting and other tactics originally derived from behind *Ninjutsu,* the art of the *Ninja*,[43] the madman before Kamiizumi arrived.

Aside: Kamiizumi Hidetsuna called his school *Shinkage* for the "black curtain" of confusion he taught his students to pull over the eyes of their opponents. This was in keeping with the dictates of *Sonshi* (Sun Tzu) that the best battles are those won *sans* fighting.

The best illustration of Kamiizumi practicing what he preached (i.e., *appreciation* into *application*) was an incident in which he disarmed a crazed sword-wielding opponent by using a single rice cake.

An enraged, sword-wielding man had seized a small child as a hostage rather than allowing himself to be apprehended by the authorities. For fear of the child being harmed, everyone gave up, deciding to wait the madman out. Everyone, that is, except for Kamiizumi.

Donning the robe of a Buddhist monk, Kamiizumi slowly and nonchalantly approached the madman and his hostage, first offering the frightened child a rice cake before then casually tossing one to the enraged man. . . .

Already confused (but not overly alarmed) by the approach of this "Buddhist monk," the madman *instinctively* reached out to catch the tossed rice cake.

As the man reached out, Kamiizumi seized hold of the man's extended arm, easily pulling the man into an inescapable *juijutsu* hold.

Rather than confronting the madman with equal or exceeding force, thereby further endangering the hostage, Kamiizumi had opted to "mind-dance" past the man's defenses. Thus he employed the following insights and ploys:

By donning the robes of a "harmless" Buddhist priest, Kamiizumi (1) caused the man to drop his guard, since he would see the "Buddhist monk" as nonthreatening, and (2) seeing a "holy man" approach-

---

43. For more on such "Samurai *Ninja*," see Dr. Lung's *The Ninja Craft* (Alpha Publications, 1997), and *Nine Halls of Death* by Dr. Haha Lung and Eric Tucker (Citadel Press, 2007).

ing him invoked whatever moral, social, and religious condition still remained in the crazed man's mind.

In addition, and perhaps most importantly, Kamiizumi recognized *the level at which his opponent was functioning* and adjusted his strategy accordingly.

Negotiators had already tried "reasoning" and then threatening the madman before Kamiizumi arrived.

Kamiizumi recognized that the enraged man was operating on a primal level. To try reasoning or even threatening such a paranoid and psychotic person would be useless, unless you could approach the man on the same primitive level at which he was stuck.

After first "calming" the man by wearing Buddhist garb, Kamiizumi then played on (1) the man's hunger urge, and (2) the instinctive way human beings snatch at anything thrown to them.[44]

> For the mediocre man knows only what is shown, without knowing how to direct his gaze toward what is hidden. —Yagu Munanori, *Heiho Koden Sho*

Like Musashi, Munenori was not a man to coast on his past achievements. Once he'd mastered the sword and numerous other martial arts weapons, Munenori took the next logical step, devoting the rest of his life to developing the unarmed combat art of *Muto* (literally "No sword").

The *mu* in Munenori's *Muto* came originally from the Chinese *wu,* meaning "no thing [*sic*]."[45]

The *to* is "sword," hence "*Muto*" . . . "No sword," referring both to the action of disarming an armed opponent when you yourself pos-

---

44. Asked by a talk show host show to "explain" his art, Bruce Lee plucked an apple from a nearby fruit bowl and tossed this apple to his startled host, who nonetheless snatched the apple from the air **without hesitating**. "That," Bruce told him, "is my art."

45. "Mu" ("No thing" and "Not this") is a popular Zen meditation. Simply sit and clear your mind (hint: imagining a placid lake helps). Anytime any thought tries to intrude, mentally repeat "*Mu*" ("Not this").

sess no weapon, and to the calm (*wa/su*) state of mind necessary to accomplish such a task.

Munenori's *Muto* specialized in doing just that: disarming armed opponents.

In a demonstration before the Togugawa Shogun, Munenori easily disarmed several would-be warriors contradicting the belief that "a man on foot has no chance against a mounted opponent." Munenori suddenly slapped the man's horse on the snout, making the horse rear up and throw off the Samurai. Munenori then easily disarmed the downed and dazed man.

Munenori's overcoming a mounted Samurai curiously qualifies as what Musashi calls "Cutting the Edges."

Unable to attack the Samurai directly, Munenori literally attacked the man's "support network," his mount.[46]

The Shogun was so delighted by Munenori's display of *Muto* prowess, he gave him the job of teaching *Muto* to Tokugawa troops.

Ultimately Munenori's "responsibilities" for the Tokugawa Shogunate would expand to include keeping an eye on enemies of the Shogun as *Metsuke* ("Censor," "Special Inspector").

While at least admirable in hindsight, Musashi, the often unwashed wandering *ronin,* was in direct contrast to Munenori's more polished ideal of *daiki taiku*: a Samurai exhibiting the virtues of honor, courage, and service to society.

"Honor" and "courage" are easy to spot in the narrative of Musashi's life. . . . That "service to society" thing, not so much.

For the most part Musashi comes across as a somewhat self-absorbed artist type, often foregoing social amenities, familial contact and connection, and even bodily hygiene, in favor of a myopic focus on perfecting his "art."

That's not to say Musashi didn't *contribute* anything to society

---

46. For more on this Musashi specialty, see "Cutting at the Edges (to Get to Their Heart!)" in Lung and Prowant's *Mind Assassins: The Dark Arts of the Asian Masters* (Citadel Press, 2010).

through the works of art he left behind, the *Gorin no sho*, for example. But while alive, bettering society was not *numero uno* on Musashi's things to do every day . . . if ever!

Still, judging by at least one definition of *daiki taiku*, Musashi, in many ways, came close:

> A man of *daiki taiku* does not at all concern himself either with things learned or with laws. In everything, there are things learned, laws, and proscription. Some-one who has attained the ultimate state brushes them aside. He does things freely, at will. Someone who goes outside the laws and acts at will is called a man of *daiki taiku*. —Hiroaki Sato, *The Sword and the Mind*

This sounds like something Nietzsche cooked up, with a little Ayn Rand thrown in to spice things up. Rightly so, for it is a call to free up the flow of our innate "Will to Power," to aspire to an impeccable point where we will no longer be bound by laws of dependency and deportment, where we see and *act*—free from the restricting false filters of Mama, Drama, and Trauma.

In Japan a person who succeeds in living such an impeccable life, independent in both thought and action, is said to possess *shibumi*, literally, "to live flawlessly."

This is the same concept we find at the core of Zen: In order for us to truly master an art, any art, we must first learn proper form and traditional technique, and then *forget those restrictions* as we reach the point in learning where our art becomes *second nature* and can be done *without conscious thought.* Thus, we transcend the "laws" that govern that particular art.

Eastern philosophy in general, and the saga of Zen in particular, is full to overflowing with tales of such "spiritual outlaws."

Recall that "transcending technique" was one of the five main principles Musashi realized through his Zen study.

Likewise, Munenori's *daiki taiku* philosophy has often been accused of having been "influenced" by Zen, of being "a confusion between swordsmanship and religious belief."[47]

Within Munenori's overall strategy for getting, and keeping, the upper hand, we easily spot several distinct tactics and techniques, all of which were, by necessity, practical and *applicable* for both battlefield encounters, as well as appropriate for the equally deadly court intrigue of the time.

Munenori's overall strategy was simple: learn to "see" your opponent's strategy while keeping your own strategy from being "seen." Thus, becoming a man of *daiki taiku* meant cultivating "The Three Types of Seeing": *Ken, Kan,* and *Hyori.*

Ken: Learning to Perceive

Ken, in Japanese, means to physically observe with the eyes. Coincidentally, the archaic English word *Ken* (to us by way of the Scots) means "to see," "to perceive," and "to understand."

Kan: Developing Insight

Kan means "insight," a deeper level of perception beyond only seeing with our two eyes. This level of seeing involves "seeing" with the mind.

You may recall Musashi's admonishment that "perception is strong, but sight is weak."

Musashi (and Munenori) are telling us that we must learn to "see" beyond just the physical, no matter how well-developed our sense of sight, learning to "read what isn't written," e.g., body language and "micro-expressions."[48]

All Masters agree: to see with only the eyes, is to "see" through *dumb*-colored glasses.

---

47. Tokitsu, 2004.

48. Unconscious facial and body "tics" that betray a person's doubt and deception.

Hyori: Mastering the Art of Deception

Hyori literally means "not being seen," but goes far beyond merely physically getting your *Ninja* on by not being seen, to developing the ability to hide your true feelings and your overall strategy of battle.

Thus, *Hyori* begins with the mastery of physical stealth,[49] eventually progressing to a more metaphorical level of hiding your intent (*wa*), keeping both your mind-set and your maneuvers a mystery to your foe.

For Musashi, the end (victory) always justified the means (strategy). Likewise, Munenori believed a man of *daiki taiku* was justified in using any and all means to accomplish his ends:

> Even if you inwardly hide the truth and outwardly carry out your stratagem, when you succeed in the end pulling your opponent into the truthful way, all deceptions become truths. —Munanori

"All deceptions become truths?" That lands somewhere between Orwell's *1984* double-speak and the ever-elusive (seemingly contradictory) Zen *balance* . . . "Things are not what they seem . . . nor are they otherwise."

Hyori soon became a catch-all meaning "double-dealing" and (deliberate) "confusion." Munenori himself once described *Hyori* as "obtaining the truth through the use of deception."

"Truth through deception," now *that* definitely qualifies as "Orwellian!" But that's hardly surprising given the fact that Munenori ran the secret police for the Tokugawa regime.

Police interrogators today still use "truth through deception" ploys, lying to a suspect (or witness), pretending to possess more information about a crime than they actually do, "minimizing" to make a suspect relax into thinking he's only been brought down to the station

---

49. Jp. *Masakatsu!*

tion for shoplifting when, in fact, it's murder-most-foul that's being investigated.[50]

Hyori teaches us to hide our intent using *kyoku* ("deception") techniques deliberately crafted to lure an opponent in by feigning weakness[51] by using such ploys as *suigetsu,* "moon reflecting on the water" (i.e., the "moon" we see reflected on the water is not the *real* moon, thus, what an enemy "sees" is only what we allow him to see). An example of this would be your infiltrating your enemy's inner circle by feigning friendship and/or by wearing a disguise.

Like Musashi, Munenori's techniques for outmaneuvering a foe both physically and psychologically were far from theoretical, having instead been gleaned the hard way from actual physical confrontations. Then came the revelation of the similarities between combat on a physical battlefield and equally deadly encounters taking place on the battlefield of the mind:

> War is war, it matters little whether your foe hides his true face behind a bulwark of pike, or a courtier's fan, whether he thrusts at you with whetted weapon or with dry wit, let no trespass go unchallenged. —Dr. Haha Lung, *Mind Control* (2006)

Early on Munenori realized that the body language (*shin-myo*) signals that announced another swordsman's intention to attack were no different from the "tells" (layman's term for "micro-expressions") he noticed when another man was lying to him.

No secret, Munenori also learned much of his strategy, both physical and psychological, from his *Ninja* "employees." Recall that some Samurai, both Musashi and Munenori fitting the bill, had no compunction about secretly adding forbidden *Ninja* tactics and technique

---

50. For a complete course on the art of interrogation, see "The Art of In-Terror-gation/Mind Assassins with a Badge" in Lung and Prowant's *Mind Assassins* (Citadel Press, 2010).

51. "When strong, appear weak" (Sun Tzu).

to their own aresenals. *Masakatsu,* remember? Morality is content to let utilitarianism jockey the pony so long as they both wind up in the winner's circle.

Six factors comprise Munenori's philosophy.

Munenori's Philosophy

Foresight. This is the ideal of every warrior, warlord, and Wall Street wizard since Sun Tzu. It's so much wiser to nip a potential problem in the bud now than to have to weed your garden later. Munenori defines "Foresight" thus:

> Foreseeing a disturbance from the various developments in the state and stopping it before it breaks out.

Chance. Chance equals opportunity. Chance also equals "Shit happens!" Chance doesn't play favorites, but it does tip its hat to the well-prepared, hence the saying, "Chance favors the prepared mind." Says Munenori:

> Seizing the chance ahead of time means carefully observing your opponent's mind and making an appropriate move just before he makes up his mind.

This is the ideal: your prior training and preparation being "triggered" by your perception (perhaps even subconscious perception) of your enemy's *shjin-myo.*

Intrigue. From political campaigning every four years, to the backbiting and backstabbing taking place every day in the workplace, we're surrounded by intrigue. Whereas the intrigue we encounter at the office every day might not be of the same often fatal *intensity* as the court intrigue of Munenori's time, its *intent* is the same: *their* advancement via *our* destruction. Thus the wise man defends himself as vigorously against the word as he does against the sword. Munenori knew the score:

Your Lord may be flanked by sycophants, who when facing him feign an air of morality, but who when looking down at the ruled give an angry glance. Such men, unless you lie low before them, will speak ill of you for something good you have done. As a result, the innocent suffer and the sinful thrive. *Understanding this is more important than the ability to judge your opponent's stratagems in a sword fight.*

The evil starters in *King Lear* come to mind, as does Iago from *Othello.* Aaron Burr, Martin Bormann, and Karl Rove also come to mind.

Practice. Despite what your high school coach might have told you, "Practice *does not* make perfect," not if your instruction and method of practice is flawed from the start. Perfection is obtainable, or at least approachable, provided we find the right mentor and the right mind-set to begin with.

Bad attitude and bad teacher to begin with . . . why bother?

Practice is discipline. Practice is discovery—both of your own strengths and the weaknesses of your opponents. Let us heed Munenori's advice on the subject:

An unpolished jewel attracts dirt and dust. A polished one doesn't become soiled even if put in the mud. Train hard and polish your mind so that it may remain so.

Strategy. Intelligence gathered mixes with intelligence innate to produce strategy. Provided that gathered intelligence is true and provided that innate intelligence remains true to itself, victory is assured.

The man with a solid plan always leads the man with a clue around by the nose. Says Munenori:

The thing to do is to force your opponent to follow your changes and by following his resultant changes to win.

Take your opportunity right after you make your opportunity.

Experience. *Experience* is another word for "application." You can theorize (appreciation phase) about something till the cows come home, but until you actually step into the ring, out on the field, *wherever* the real action is taking place and the real blood is being spilled, only then, when forced to *apply* your theory and strategy, only then will you get real-life experience.

You *won?* Good experience. You *lost?* Great experience. Losing prevents you from getting "cocky" (as winners are prone to do) and makes you (1) study even harder, and (2) pay even more attention in order to avoid getting your ass kicked again next time: Says Munenori:

> The ability to speak eloquently of the mind may not mean enlightenment on the subject. Even if you hold forth on water, your mouth does not become wet. Even if you speak eloquently of fire, your mouth doesn't become hot. You cannot know the real water and real fire without touching them; you cannot know them by explaining them in books. Likewise, even if you speak eloquently of food, hunger will not be cured. The ability to speak is not enough for knowing the subject at hand. . . . As long as they do not behave as they preach, they have yet to know the mind. Until such person explores the mind in himself and knows it fully, the matter will remain unclear.

Nietzsche said, "Do the thing and you have the power." Having experienced something firsthand, even if you fail, provided you *survive,* you come away a better person, better able to succeed next time. The Samurai creed: "Nine times down, ten times up!"

Therefore, even when you practice, practice with realism. *See* (visualize) not only the outcome, but try to feel the actual emotions (trepidation, fear, excitement, then elation) you're likely to feel during the battle to come.

Remember: practice *does not* make perfect. Only perfect practice leads us closer to perfection.

* * *

Your confidence is your enemy's confusion.

Your enemy is never so satisfied as when he sees *you* confused and stumbling about, seemingly without a clue to life in general and to what your smirking enemy is planning in particular.

On the other hand, when you exude confidence (even if only convincingly acting the part), your enemy becomes first confused, then frightened.

This is why Sun Tzu tells us, "When strong, appear weak." The weaker (and more confused) we appear, the more it emboldens our enemy. And I think we've already established how dangerous *overconfidence* can be, huh?

Confidence (yours) and confusion (his) are intricately connected. They *rise* in equal proportion: with your confidence increasing as you deliberately raise your enemy's confusion. Conversely, as you watch your enemy's confusion increase, your confidence cannot but exhibit a corresponding increase.

Specific techniques for increasing your own confidence while simultaneously increasing your enemy's confusion will be revealed in the section that follows on *"100 Secrets of the Samurai."*

> *"If confidence is indeed 'half the battle,' then to undermine the enemy's confidence is more than the other half, because it gains the fruits without an all-out fight."*
> **—Captain Sir Basil Liddell-Hart, 1944**

SAN-SHIN: THE SWORD WITH THREE MINDS

> *"There is that which I allow you to see and there is that which I keep hidden from you. Together, these make up a third which you cannot possibly imagine!"*
> **—The Answers of Attila**

When Musashi fought and defeated *kusarigama* expert Shishido, it was the first time Musashi had faced off against such a weapon: a razor-edged sickle with several feet of weighted, entangling chain attached to its handle. Not only the blade of this weapon was deadly, but you could also be struck by the weight at the end of its snapping chain, and/or become caught—the chain wrapping around your arm or foot, entangling you until the sickle-blade could finish you off.

In the hands of a Master—like Shishido—the chain could even wrap around your sword, jerking it free from your hand, leaving you defenseless!

His *katana* at the ready, Musashi drew his shorter *wakisaki*[52] and began twirling it above his head, mirroring Shishido's own whirling chain.

But Musashi wasn't concentrating on Shishido's chain, he was watching the man's face. . . . And the second Musashi saw a flicker of confusion pinch his opponent's brow, that was the instant Musashi's short sword leaped from his hand and buried itself in Shishido's chest!

Another half second, and Musashi had "bridged the gap" between them, finishing Shisido with a single slash of his *katana*.

Shishido died wondering, "What went wrong?"

What "went wrong"[53] was that the *kusarigama* Master had fallen victim to Musashi's use of the *San-shin*[54] ploy.

"*San-shin*" can be translated as "The Sword with Three Minds." In actuality, we have two swords (or two ploys) that, when used in concert, create *a third unseen possibility.* Right, a case of the third being greater than the sum of its parts.

To his credit, Shishido has mastered the full capabilities of his own weapon. During his many duels he'd not only fought many Samurai armed with a *katana* and a few armed with both *katana* and *wakizashi.* So, finding himself facing off against Miyamoto Musashi, already renowned for his "unorthodox" style (read: *trickery!*), Shishido knew

---

52. Sometimes called a *kodachi.*

53. From Shishido's perspective at least. From Musashi's perspective, things couldn't have gone better!

54. Experts disagree as to whether it was actually called "*San-shin*" before *Musashi used it.*

Musashi might resort to using his short sword to guard and parry against the chain while attacking with his long sword. . . .

In Shishido's mind he had both "A" (long sword) and "B" (short sword) covered. . . . But what he hadn't factored in was some of that Musashi math where "A" + "B" = some sort of never-been-seen-before "C."

As Musashi's short sword drew Shishido's attention (that strange twirling motion again), *Is Musashi making fun of my weapon?* Shishido wondered.

Confusion left just enough of a gap in Shishido's defense for *hesitation* to let *Death* get his foot in the door.

Shishido would not make *that* mistake again. (Heh-heh-heh.)

Musashi's sword (actually two swords, the long and the short) has "three minds," thus:

- He could use it for parry and blocking;
- He could use it for cutting and stabbing; and
- He could use it in an *unorthodox* manner, as he did, by throwing it like a spear, impaling his opponent, opening the way for his *coup de grace.*

Finding unusual uses for everyday objects requires that we bypass what's known as "object fixedness," the tendency of human beings to see only a singular use for an object. Great artists and great *street fighters* are known for their ability to overcome this object fixedness: "It's not just a piece of marble; it's a beautiful statue wanting to come out!" . . . "It's not just a brick . . . it's my one chance to survive this vicious mugging."

The ancient adage that "we are limited only by our imagination" still holds true. All too often we fall victim to "object fixedness," not only when dealing with things, but with people, as well.

In the same way a pencil can suddenly "transform" into a deadly dagger should we find ourselves in a kill-or-be-killed survival situation, so, too, the people we might at first glance dismiss as "useless" all have hidden, untapped resources and talents that can be put to good use.

Now, lest you get to thinking Dr. Lung suddenly grew a naïve "optimism bone," keep in mind that anyone and *everyone* on this planet is also a potential stumbling block, blockhead, and potential *enemy* blocking your path to safety, succor, and ultimate success.

Thus, the more we know about ourselves, our (potential) enemy, and our environment—Sun Tzu's "Three Knows"—the better our chances of surviving to see another day.

As with everyday objects, the people in our lives (yeah, and often standing in our way!) have *numerous* uses (and abuses!) depending on how well we can "read" them. But, as with all things in life, people have two sides, the obvious and the hidden.

In Japan this *yin-yang* division is known as *omote*, what things *appear* like "on the surface," and *ura*, "that which resides just *below* the surface."

Ura is used interchangeably with *oku*, which implies there is more "depth" to a thing, situation, or person than at first might appear. Think iceberg.

In Shingon Buddhism, as with some other variations of Japanese religion, *omote* and *ura* manifest as *kenshi* and *mikkyo* respectively, the "exoteric" overt, more easily seen aspects of spiritual practice, as compared to the more "esoteric," arcane and more obscure practices.

We see (or *don't* see) this same division in the martial arts, where schools give overt and obvious training to all students, while reserving the teaching of "secret" technique to the advanced and "chosen" few.

Zen Master Takuan saw these "inner" and "outer" aspects of training as "wheels of the same cart" (Ratti and Westbrook, 1973).

Chinese strategists such as Sun Tzu and Cao Cao referred to this as *ching* and *ch'i*, i.e., orthodox force (think Napoleon and Patton) and unorthodox force (think Che Guevara and Robert Rogers).[55]

There is a place for both *ching and ch'I*, whether our fight be on

---

55. For a complete course on American Colonial guerilla strategist Major Robert Rogers on "Nineteen Rules of War," see Lung and Prowant's *Ultimate Mind Control* (Citadel Press, 2011).

the battlefield or in the board room: seeing us arrive at the meeting with the expected *ching*—wooden sword (or pile of files, as the case may be)—our opponent assumes an orthodox (*ching*) battle . . . thus we startle him with an unexpected *ch'i* maneuver.

On the other hand, Bruce Lee maintained that overcoming an enemy with an advanced, complicated technique is not the epitome of skill. Rather, defeating an enemy with a *simple and basic* move shows Mastery. Thus expecting trickery of every sort, expecting us to surprise him with a novel *ch'i* move (as Musashi did Shishido), we instead take him out with "the ol' one-two."

It is perhaps ironic (or just "Zen!") that the greatest "secret" to the martial arts is . . . *there is no secret!* Just (1) a lot of hard work—what our Chinese brothers call "*Kung-fu*"—and (2) our taking the time (yeah, a little *meditation* wouldn't hurt) to slow down long enough to understand the "inner workings" (*okogi*)[56] of the particular thing we've chosen to study.

From people—that lover who is just *too perfect*, to that "short" sword Shishido underestimated (that soon made "short work" of him, heh-heh-heh)—*underestimating* our enemy (or anything our enemy might use against us) puts us in a dangerous, deficit position.

You see only a doorman and an angry-at-the-world woman working down at the DMV. *Your enemy* contracted that same *hooker* with a hidden camera to catch you in a compromising positioned, or two.

On the more mundane side: what about all that "fine print" and lawyer-talk paragraphs in that contract you just signed?

Yes, the thought of all the hidden trips and traps, minefields and minions an enemy can place in your path can be overwhelming.

But we need not be overwhelmed so long as we follow some of the rules Musashi learned early on:

- *Every hand's a winner, and every hand's a loser*: Both Kenny Rogers and Musashi realized that it's not what you've been given in

---

56. Sometimes translated "inner *mysteries*."

life . . . it's what you do with what you've been given in life that secures your freedom and success. Oh yeah, Spartacus, Nietzche, and Ayn Rand all wrote in blood on this same page. Every*body* has some use . . . even the body you bury in your enemy's basement.

- *Learn what your enemy knows, and then master what you know*: When they offer you the choice *between* the carrot or the stick . . . take the stick. Then as soon as their back is turned, use the stick to *take* their carrot!

- *There is an "outside" and an "inside" to all things*: If you don't want your *insides* spilled outside, you'd best get *inside* your enemy's head P. D.Q.! What your enemy allows you to see is never as potentially useful as what he keeps hidden. For every one thing he shows you, he keeps ten hidden, any one of which, uncovered, can aid in your victory. Likewise, show your enemy what you want him to see. Then, prepare a "deeper" level of supposedly hidden information you *want* him to discover—this is called "misinformation."

The Dead Dog Ploy is said to have been created (or at least perfected) by the *thuggee* strangler cult of India.

Having killed a traveler (per instruction of their goddess *Kali*), these thugs would first bury the corpse, then toss a dead dog (or other animal) into the grave before filling the rest in.

When British authorities were led to such a grave by dogs, digging a couple feet down, they would discover the rotting dog carcass and not dig down any further (assuming that it was this carcass that had "alerted" the cadaver dogs).[57]

In modern day, hide whatever you don't want the enemy (be that "enemy" your nosy porn collection–hating wife, your boss, the IRS, or the FBI?) to find under an initial layer of "misinformation" you *want*

---

57. For the complete history and training methods of the ancient killer cult of Kali, see Dr. Lung's *The Ancient Art of Strangulation* (Paladin Press, 1995).

them to find. Odds are, they'll be satisfied and too busy patting themselves on the back to "dig" any deeper.

In any martial art, you begin by learning the basics. *Most* never progress beyond this point. Despite what non-initiates might think, even the awarding of the coveted "Black Belt" doesn't confer "Master" status on a karate or kung-fu practitioner. A Black Belt merely acknowledges your ability to properly teach and pass on your respective art.

Few students, especially in today's hectic world, have the time, temperament, or tenaciousness to devote to unraveling the "inner mysteries" of anything.[58]

Realizing that things and people have more than one use (*sen-shin*) opens the door to endless possibilities, filling your arsenal to overflowing.

"Sen nichi no keiko o tan to shi, man nichi no keiko o ran to su."[59]
—**The Scroll of Water,** *Gorin no sho*

IRYOKO: MASTERING THE ART OF INTIMIDATION

"My power proceeds from my reputation, and my reputation from the victories I have won. My power would fall if I were not to support it with more glories and more victories. Conquest has made me what I am; only conquest can maintain me."
—*Napoleon*

For all the duels Musashi fought, for all the bodies of the slow and the slain littering his path to greatness, there were a thousand

---

58. Unless it's unraveling the "secrets" of "progressing" to the next level of their favorite video game . . .

59. "A thousand days to learn. Ten thousand days to polish."

gunslingers, huh! *sword*-slingers—a lump in their throat and testicles suddenly drawn up into their body—who lowered their gaze and quickly stepped to the other side of the street when they saw *Kensei* approach!

How often has Dr. Lung told you, "Reputation spills less blood." *Reputation* is power. Or the *lack* of power you possess.

When people talk about you behind your back, at least they're afraid to say it to your face, huh? Their reluctance to confront you face-to-face shows that they're at least a little *intimidated* by your power.

A quick review: There are five types of power:

- *Love and Respect Power:* Based on how much you are loved and respected by others.
- *Reward Power:* Aka "the Carrot," based on your ability to manipulate others by dispensing rewards.
- *Coercive Power:* Aka "the Stick," based on your willingness to threaten and, when need be, to physically punish others.
- *Expert Power:* Based on your having access to valuable skills, unique abilities, or special intelligence.
- *Position Power:* Based on a person's recognized and agreed-upon right to issue commands and make demands of others.[60]

At various times, various people hold one or more of these types of power over us, while we ourselves may likewise hold the similar or same power(s) over those subordinate to us.

For example, *parents* generally receive "Love and Respect" off the top if only because of their "position" over their children. But, depending on the severity of your upbringing, your parents might have also freely wielded both "the Carrot" (allowances, that trip to Disney World) and/or "the Stick" power ("You are *so* grounded for life!") over you in order to bribe or else threaten you into behaving.

---

60. For a complete discussion of "The Five Types of Power (and How to Get Some)," see Dr. Lung's *Ultimate Mind Control* (Citadel Press, 2011).

Of course, our parents always "knew best" . . . This gives them "Expert Power" over us.

And, let's be honest, all five of these types of "power" pretty much come down to someone wielding power over us because of our *fear* of what will happen if we don't obey.

Even with "Love and Respect Power," there is still the underlying "threat" of what will happen if that love and respect is unexpectedly withdrawn or deliberately withheld.

Sure, you "love" and "respect" your country . . . just see how much "love" and "respect" you get in return next time you forget to file your income taxes!

Of course, true "Love and Respect Power" is unconditional. We love and respect our parents first and foremost because they are our parents. Likewise our teachers and other authority figures. Even when we don't necessarily agree with them, we still obey them out of love and respect (some might read that as "duty"). Even when the "love" might wane, we still "respect the office, respect the rank" enough to give it its due.

Despite his reputation as a ruthless and heartless SOB, Niccòlo Machiavelli wrestled with whether a prince should rule from a position of power based on love or fear.

An astute observer, Machiavelli fully understood the importance of keeping *fear* firmly fixed in our foe's heart.

In Chapter XVII of his masterpiece *The Prince* (1513), Machiavelli questions, and then answers, whether it is better (and by "better" he means "safer") for a prince (or any leader for that matter) to be loved or feared by his subjects:

> And as to the question whether it is better to be loved rather than feared, or feared rather than loved: Some might answer that we should want both; but since love and fear can scarce exist together, forced to choose between the two, let us decide it is far *safer* to be feared than loved. For can we not agree that men are for the

most part ungrateful, fickle and false? They study to avoid danger and are greedy for gain. Devoted to you while you hold position to heap benefits upon them. Eager to shed blood, sacrifice their lands and their lives and their children in your cause, loud when danger is still distant, in your hour of need they turn from you.

One of Machiavelli's many nicknames was *not* "Mr. Optimistic"!

However, in their haste to paint Machiavelli the imp of immorality, many biographers neglect to point out how, in *The Prince*, Machiavelli is careful to draw the distinction between being *feared* and being *hated*.

Evidently twenty years did little to improve Machiavelli's overall assessment of man, nor alter his initial conclusion that being *feared* was *safer* than depending on capricious love. Thus, in 1531, in Book III of his *Discourses*, Machiavelli tells us:

> Men are mainly motivated by two things: love or fear. Therefore a Prince either makes himself loved or makes himself feared. Ultimately, a man who makes himself feared is better served and obeyed than a man who believes himself loved.

Machiavelli's choosing of fear over love sounds reasonable if for no other reason than that with a single *selfish* act love can be transformed into fear, even hate. Yet many *selfless* acts are required to turn fear into love.[61]

> The ugly truth is revealed that fear is the foundation of obedience. —Sir Winston Churchill, *The River War* (1899)

Musashi was no stranger to using *all five* of the five types of power. During his colorful, and surprisingly long life, Musashi handled all five as adroitly as he wielded his physical blades.

---

61. For a complete discussion of the philosophy of Machiavelli, see "The Machiavelli Method" in Lung and Prowant's *Ultimate Mind Control* (Citadel Press, 2011).

That he enjoyed the love and respect of his admirers, his adopted son, the *Daimyos* he Samuraied for, and the fellow warriors he fought beside is no secret.

At the most basic, Musashi wielded both "the Carrot" and "the Stick" (sometimes literally!) since he literally held in his hand(s) the power of life and death. This would also qualify as his possessing (using?) coercive power.

And while Musashi never sought wealth and power, in his role as *sensei*, he would have wielded great power over his students. And we should also note that, at various times, Musashi held actual military "rank" (i.e., position) under the various *Daimyos* he served.

Early on in his life, his reputation already on the rise, his "intimidation factor" began increasing exponentially.

"*Intimidation*," as used in Black Science, doesn't necessarily mean keeping your enemies quaking 24/7 (although that *would* be tempting!). "Intimidation," as used in a mind control context, is a tangible presence, our exuding an aura of control, confidence, and command we compose from a combination of craft[62] and charisma.

In his excellent *Control Freaks: Who They Are and How to Stop Them from Running Your Life* (1991), Gerald W. Piaget lists three factors necessary for being "an effective intimidator" as having (1) a reputation, (2) a set of intimidating moves, and (3) a willingness to ruthlessly squash anyone who gets in your way.[63]

Can there be any doubt Musashi possessed Piaget's three intimidation criteria in abundance?

Three Intimidation Criteria

Maintain a reputation. Reputation means creating an image of invincibility that makes sure everybody knows what a bad-ass you really

---

62. "Craft" as both "skill" and "cunning."
63. Machiavelli would have loved Gerald Piaget?

are, whether on the battlefield, in the board room, or, yes, even in the bedroom.

While the most dependable reputations are carved with the blade, those reputations molded from a steaming pile of bullshit are often just as effective.

Your "reputation" should be based on authentic accounts of your past conquests: on the battlefield, in the board room, in the bedroom. On the other hand, *Black Science*–wise, your reputation can be completely fabricated: strategic *dis*information designed to hesitate, hogtie, and hoodwink your competition. Remember: reputation spills less blood.

There's no denying that, early on in his life, Musashi established his "reputation" as a bad-ass.

Killing his first man in a duel at age thirteen, Musashi was then well on his way to establishing his reputation as someone not to be messed with.

In many ways, Musashi reminds us of another precocious (predatory) thirteen-year-old who also "made his bones," thus his reputation, at a early age: young Henry McCarty of Brooklyn, New York, better known as William Bonney, better known still as "Billy the Kid." But, unlike that infamous Wild West wild child, who stabbed a man to death in a bar fight, Musashi's age-thirteen duel, if not "sanctioned" by polite Japanese society, was accepted as part-'n'-parcel of the Samurai ethics.

Acquire a set of intimidating moves. Once you decide on intimidation as your overall strategy, you must acquire tactics and techniques. "Talk the talk and walk the walk" that makes others "see" just how formidable a force you really are. Either that, or you have to learn how to "fake it till you can make it" by ratcheting up your "bluff game" via the *illusion* of "invincibility" you weave around yourself.

Recall our discussion on just how *untrustworthy* the *average* person's everyday perceptions are.[64]

---

64. See also "*Jing Gong*: How to Train Your Senses," in Lung and Prowant's *Ultimate Mind Control* (Citadel, 2011).

First, how many times do we have to tell you: *Stop being "average"!* Second, remember that perception, no matter how screwed up, is *reality*. If you *make* your enemies *"see"* you as a force to be reckoned with, they will then act (cower!) accordingly.

There are those who maintain that Musashi was a *savant* whom Mother Nature "gifted" with the skill to kill, and to do so with flourish.

Others give Musashi his due, judging him to have been a most observant student, learning early on from his sword-master father, and from any Samurai who crossed his path.

The truth of the matter? Probably a combination of gene, spleen, and keen insight allowed the young Musashi to live long enough to become the older Musashi.

As for that "set of intimidating moves" . . . have you ever even read Musashi's *Gorin no sho*?

Learn to "crush" the opposition. In order to be truly intimidating, every now and then you have to actually "put up" in order to "shut up" your opposition. In other words, you have to openly crush someone like a bug in order to send a clear message to all the other cockroaches lurking in the shadows, eyeing *your table* for their next meal.

This "crushing" harkens back to those *Sons of Brutus*: defeating your enemy, *with finality*, the first time.

In the same way you must always be quick to reward loyalty and efficiency within *your* pride, so, too, occasionally, you'll need to snatch one of the indolent and infirm from your enemy's herd, making a glaring example of them in order to encourage the rest of the herd to step lively!

Swift reward and swifter punishment lead to loyalty and lasting results. Acting in this way reinforces your already fierce reputation for ruthlessness, dissuading other predators from testing the temper of your tooth and nail.

Adhere to Machiavelli's admonition from *The Prince*[65] that "men are either to be treated kindly, or else utterly crushed. . . ."

---

65. Chapter III and again in Chapter VII.

Reward all those wise enough to join you, utterly crush all who dare oppose you, and do so in so savage a manner as to completely cower any others who might dream of resisting your will! —Attila the Hun[66]

RIN-ROKU: SECRETS OF THE SIXTH RING

"We must hold our minds alert and receptive to the application of unglimpsed methods and weapons."
—*General Douglas MacArthur, 1931*

Musashi organized his opus *Gorin no sho* as "A Book of Five Rings" for a reason.

Much of Eastern thought in general and Eastern religious thought in particular is based upon the ancient Chinese concept of *Wu-Hsing*, "The Five Elements": for the Japanese, they were Earth, Fire, Water, Wind, Void.[67]

Across the centuries, these "Five Elements" have been associated with every aspect of life, as they are considered the basic building blocks of all existence.

From traditional Chinese medicine to military strategy, from the turning of the seasons to the turning of the human mind, correspondences—pro and con—have been discovered for these Five Elements.

By understanding the interactions of these Five Elements (in their various manifestations) we can "add" or "subtract" needed element "influences," the way we would add or subtract something to our diet in order to gain or lose weight, or otherwise balance our system.

There's nothing mysterious or complicated in this: confronted with an *angry, shouting* person, realizing that both the feeling of "anger"

---

66. This passage from Attila's "Answers" is sometimes referred to as the "Conqueror's Dictum" . . . which Attila did and did well!

67. Also called "Metal," and also called "Wood," in Chinese.

and the behavior of "shouting" are governed by the "element" *Void/Wood*, we can choose to confront him forcefully with a "fire" response (e.g., derisively laughing in his face), perhaps escalating his anger, or else attempt to distract and diffuse him through humor (another form of laughter).

Studying the Five Elements also allows us to find the most opportune time to approach him, for example, a Void/Wood–dominated person is strongest in the early morning hours, not the best time to approach him if hoping to convince him to come over to your side.

In Japan *Wu-hsing* is called *Gojo-Goyoku*, "The Five Weaknesses." Needless to say, appreciation and application of these Five Weaknesses are required study for both Jinja and for think-outside-the-box Samurai strategists like Musashi and Munenori.

In calling his masterpiece "A Book of Five Rings," in organizing his writings into five so-named chapters, Musashi left no stone (or element) unturned in his search for, and understanding of, how these Five Elements interact, reinforcing or else interdicting one another.

For example, *Wu-hsing* theory states that Metal destroys Wood. In turn Wood destroys Earth. Thus, faced with a Wood-dominated personality, Musashi was free to counter with a Fire-based maneuver.

Facing a Water-inspired attack, Musashi could "add" Wood-influenced factors, drawing his opponent into a Wood action, one easily countered by Musashi's Fire technique.

Thus, by appreciating and then applying all Five Elements, studying himself to ensure he did not become "dominated" by one or more of these elements, Musashi had at his disposal a "sixth" ring of power.

Buddhist philosophy recognizes what they call "The Six Aggregates." According to this, our five senses bounce back and forth, first one dominating, then another, switching back and forth from one another so quickly, so seamlessly, as to give the impression of a "sixth" aggregate, which, according to Buddhism, we mistake for being "us."

In other words, according to Buddhist philosophy at least, "you" and "I" don't really exist. What exists are the five senses bouncing around at a blinding speed, giving us the impression of there being a permanent, unchanging "us" (in the same way a spinning fan blade gives the impression of being solid, when it it actually made up of separate blades).

Similarly, when we master the full use of our five "known" senses, to the indolent it can often appear we possess a "sixth sense" of ESP.[68]

In the same way, by mastering the "Five Elements," to the point of naming the chapters of the *Gorin no sho* thus, Musashi created a "Sixth Ring," a perfect synthesis of the original five.

In the same way, this "Sixth Ring" of knowledge, such as it is, can seamlessly blend with the previous eight of "The Nine Secret Ways" to form an impenetrable defense strategy.

"By discovering the enemy's dispositions and remaining
invisible ourselves, we can keep our forces concentrated while
the enemy must be divided. We can form a single united body,
while the enemy must split up into fractions. Hence, there will
be a whole pitted against separate parts of the whole, which
means that we shall be many to the enemy's few."
—Sun Tzu

---

68. For a complete training course on activating your own "ESP," see "Making Sense of the Sixth Sense," in Dr. Lung's *Mind Penetration* (Citadel Press, 2007).

IV.

Modern-Day Musashi

"A discipline from the art of warriors can survive in modern society only if it answers to an implicit expectation on the part of society, either a practical one or one that promotes a certain cultural identity."
—**Kenji Tokitsu, from the days when he was wading through swamps, in** *Miyamoto Musashi: His Life and Writings*

THE FACT THAT Musashi initially fought against the rise of the Tokugawa, only to later embrace their rule, speaks to his adaptability.

We first find him fighting in the ranks of the army of the anti-Tokugawa Ashikaga forces at the Battle of Sakigahara, a slaughter that saw over 70,000 slain and the losers, including Musashi, being hunted down like animals.

Musashi survived, of course, and less than ten years later, we find an older, wiser Musashi fighting on the side of the Tokugawa at the seige of Osaka castle against the last holdout of the Ashikaga family he'd once served.

This is not to imply Musashi was the type of man to give his loyalty lightly, quite the opposite. From the days when he was wading through swamps trying to stay one step ahead of those Tokugawa assassins, to the day he stood advising the Tokugawa how best to storm Osaka castle,[1] Musashi served with distinction whomever he served. *Bushido.*

Musashi was nothing if not a survivor. And a survivor can never be a survivor unless they early on take "Adapt or die!" as their credo.

Keep in mind that Musashi was born during Japan's aptly named *Sengoku*, "Warring States Period," roughly 1467 through 1615, when the Tokugawa finally reestablished the office of *Shogun.*

Specifically, Musashi was born during the reign of Hidayoshi Toyotomi, which lasted from 1582 (the death of Oda Nobunaga) until Toyotomi's own death in 1603, after which the Tokugawa began asserting power, culminating in their triumph at Sekigahara.

For Musashi, as for many rogues and *ronin* of the day, the rise of the Tokugawa meant the end of much of Samurai "independence" (read: wanderlust and wanton war-mongering!).

The coming of the Tokugawa curbed the rampant power of the other great Samurai families, preventing them from fielding massive armies against one another. Correspondingly, this crackdown by the Tokugawa led to (1) an increase in crime, and (2) the emergence of special interest groups, financial concerns, and corporations, all of whom fielded their own cadre of specialized fighters.

It has been argued (accused!) that the Tokugawa put *business* before *Bushido.* However much the truth of this allegation, the historical fact is that business did benefit greatly from the unification of Japan under the Tokugawa's one rule.

It's a no-brainer: it's a lot more difficult to raise crops and animals for market when you (1) have rival armies stomping back and forth across your fields, burning your markets, and (2) passing armies constantly killing off—or else shanghaiing—you, your field hands, your friends, and your family members!

As in all times and climes, unless *you* are the one selling the bludgeons and blades and bombs, war is bad for business.

---

1. Popular lore has it the castle was finally infiltrated by *Ninja* in the Tokugawa employ.

As a result of the "Tokugawa peace," business thrived, and Japan saw a corresponding rise in the influence of its merchant class, to the denigration of the Samurai as the "ruling class."

Thus, the days when stalwart Samurai sought out *Daimyo* to serve were becoming fewer and further between. As a result, many Samurai literally hung up their swords and became farmers or craftsmen.

Other Samurai stayed *ronin*, hiring themselves out to the highest bidder, some eventually stooping to terrorizing townsfolk and farmers for their next meal.

By this time all those *yamabushi* "mountain warriors" had either died out, been killed out, or finally got a little meditation in their lives and mellowed out. Whichever, they no longer posed the kind of threat to the new regime as they had in earlier times.

Of course *Ninja* still lurked in the shadows (it's in their job description!), but the days of the mighty clans of *Shinoi Ninja* ruling whole swathes of Iga and Koga Provinces were likewise coming to an end—most having already been decimated by Nobunaga and Toyotomi.

That's not to say the rise of the Tokugawa didn't also bring new opportunities for out-of-work *ronin* and *Ninja* holding up signs reading: "Will cut throats for soup!"

More and more *ronin* hired out as *yojimbo* bodyguards protecting merchants and their goods. Soon *hatamoto-yakko* "specialized fighting units" began popping up in major Japanese cities. These were basically private security hired by guilds and financial corporations (*za*) to protect goods and workers (in that order), often from competing *hatamoto-yakko* hired by rival *za*.

As trade became increasingly policed by the ever-growing Tokugawa bureaucracy, merchants increasingly made deals with *wako*,[2] pirates raiding along the Chinese coast and bringing in forbidden foreign goods from other ports of call.

In response to increasing violence in the streets from clashes

---

2. Chinese, meaning "sons" (*ko*) of "Japan" (*wa*).

between rival *hatamoto-yakko*, corruption within *za* houses, and the usual increase in lawlessness that accompanies prosperity, the Tokugawa created one of the world's first truly comprehensive and effective police forces. . . . Right, made up mostly of out-of-work Samurai (with not a few *Ninja* thrown in for added expertise).

Now comes the question of which came first, the chicken or the egg?

It's true that increased fighting between rival *hatamoto-yakko* (collectively known as *Otokodate*) led to the Tokugawa regime passing a law banning anyone except Samurai from sporting swords. This, in turn, led to many cadre designing *and disguising* their own weapons, some crafted from innocuous objects (long metal smoking pipes, for example), others ingeniously disguised as everyday objects that would elude the scrutiny of even the most nosy Tokugawa *Metsuke*.

Metsuke ("censors") were the eyes and ears (and, when necessary, *bludgeons*) of the Tokugawa regime. Ratti and Westbrook call them the "spiritual forebear of the secret police" of Japan.[3]

Indeed, the "policing" efforts of the Tokugawa had none of the separation of "domestic" police and "military" spheres of influence we've come to expect today.

Having gained power, the Tokugawa planned to remain in power. As a result, they spent a lot of time spying on their own people.

Given Japan's history (some might venture "penchant") for court intrigue, religious rebellion, and *Ninja* lurking behind every sliding screen, this was not so much "paranoia" as it was "practical."

Soon after coming to power, Iayesu Tokugawa appointed *Ninja Jonin* Hanzo Hattori to his staff of advisors. Hattori's *Ninja* then became not only Iayasu's bodyguard (disguised as "gardeners" and "servants"), but also added their "cutting edge" expertise to the Tokugawa's growing "police" presence.

In addition, Iayesu sponsored Yagyu Munenori's *Yagyu-ryu* school of *kendo*. Students from this school then went on to form "police," tasked

---

3. *Secrets of the Samurai: The Martial Arts of Feudal Japan* (Boston: Tuttle, 1973).

with gathering intelligence on the Japanese themselves. Later these activities would be expanded under the military into the *Kempeitai,* expanding into an international spying agency, accused of *Gestapo*-like behavior during WWII.

"The chicken or the egg" comes in when we consider: was there really so much intrigue and corruption going on that the Tokugawa needed to take such extensive intelligence-gathering precautions, *or* did increased surveillance and government intrusiveness encourage secretiveness and skullduggery on the part of the Japanese people in general, and by the various (already) shadowy cadre already in play in particular?

Consider: this same time period saw the formalization of Japan's version of the "Mafia" known as *Yakuza,*[4] with Japanese criminals in general becoming more "organized" in response to increased policing by the Tokugawa.

Za headsmen often hired these nascent *yakuza,*[5] as bodyguards and as street fighters.[6]

Some outlaws from back in the early Tokugawa days are still seen today in Japan as "Robin Hoods." For example, outlaw chieftain Jiro-cho, aka "Number One Boss" of the Tokaido Highwaymen, thumbed his nose at Tokugawa authorities despite concerted efforts to capture (and/or assassinate) him. Jirocho, Japan's Jesse James, a gambler and highwayman, feared by all rival gangs, eventually took to hiring himself and his gang out to "protect" the caravans at the various guilds and corporations travelling to market up and down his Tokaido Highway.

Chicken and the egg: Increased criminal activity brought calls from honest folk for more protection. More protection came in the form of

---

4. The name means "8-9-3," the worst-possible score in a popular underworld game called *hanafuds* ("flower cards"). This is analogous to Eastern criminals tattooing themselves with the words "Born to Lose."

5. For a complete exposé of the techniques, tricks, and terror tactics of modern-day *Yakuza,* see "8-8-3" in Dr. Lung's *Mind Penetration* (Citadel Press, 2007), and "The Yakuza Strike!" in Lung and Prowant's *Mind Assassins* (Citadel Press, 2010).

6. Ratti and Westbrook, 1973: 150.

the Tokugawa government cracking down on *any* kind of traffic, even making it harder for merchants to get their goods to market. Less goods, more demand. More demand, higher prices. More costly goods means more profit for any willing to gamble on ill-gotten gain.

Despite this, *Za* continued to turn a profit during Tokugawa times, so much so that by the end of the Tokugawa Era in 1876, these *za*, known as the *Zaibatsu*, had formed a cartel controlling all major industries in Japan.

Zaibatsu bosses also bankrolled a multitude of nationalistic secret societies, most (in)famous, the *Genyoshakai* ("Black Ocean Society") and *Kokurkykai* ("Black Dragon Society"),[7] groups responsible for all the pre-WWI (Black Ocean) and pre-WWII (Black Dragon) espionage and chicanery benefiting Japan.[8]

This same strain of Japanese espionage continued after WWII, well into the Cold War, with former *Kempeitai* officers and Black Dragon operatives literally slipping the hangman's noose by convincing the Allies they, too, literally saw red—"red" as in *Communists*.

Just as they'd successfully done in Germany and Italy, in post-WWII Japan the OSS (and, after 1947, the CIA) recruited these former members of the *Kempeitai*. U.S. intelligence also employed former administrators and agents of Japan's "Thought Police," all in the name of fighting Communism.[9]

Just as they'd forgiven the German Gestapo and intelligentsia needed to help augment America's arms race with the Russians, so, too, U.S. intelligence first forgave then gave visas to Japanese "Mind Control" experts who promised to aid the United States in its *undeclared* "Mind War" with the Soviets and with China.

Shadowy cadre included the mysterious *Hai Wai*, lorded over by

---

7. Aka "The Amur Society," named for the Amur (Ch. *Heilong*) River separating China and Russia.

8. For the complete history *and* training methods of these master Japanese spies, see "Asian Arts of Espionage" in Lung and Prowant's *Mind Warrior: Strategies for Total Mental Domination* (Citadel Press, 2010).

9. See Kaplan and Dubrow, 1986.

the equally mysterious Professor Fujisawa,[10] who claimed as one of its most-promising Western alumni none other than Lee Harvey Oswald.[11]

What all these shadow cadre have in common is that they all trace themselves back, legitimate lineage or wishful thinking, to the political restructuring and resultant Machiavellian machinations taking place in early Tokugawa times in general, and often to martial Masters like Musashi in particular.

Whatever their particular political and/or financial agenda, all these groups tipped their topknots to Japan's *Kensei* Sword Saint, if not through actual physical lineage of Master-to-student, then through a "spiritual" or "philosophical" lineage.

At the start of the Tokugawa Period, everybody and their *Sensei* were looking for "the Edge" over rivals real and imagined, as is ever the way of the warrior, even in times that *appear* peaceful.

Tokugawa times were anything *but* peaceful, no matter how *seemingly placid* those times appeared on the surface.

The simple fact was the Tokugawa had seized the whole pie, leaving everyone else to scramble for, and squabble over, the crumbs.

As the great Samurai families and clans *openly* exercised less and less power, special interest groups and "protective leagues" like the *Kyokau* ("Hero Hosts" militia) sprang up to protect their towns and neighborhoods from roving bands of out-of-work *ronin*. These "commonfolk" had their own code of conduct comparable to the Samurai *Bushido*, known as *kitkotsu,* dedicated to defending commoners against renegades and rogue *ronin.*

Chicken and the egg again: Tokugawa authorities thought it prudent to keep an eye on the training of Samurai, let alone training non-Samurai. Because of such increased scrutiny, clandestine schools of martial arts also flourished underground.[12]

---

10. See "Japan: Silk and Steel" in *Mind Penetration: The Ancient Art of Mental Mastery* by Dr. Haha Lung (Citadel Press, 2007).

11. See "Oswald and the Sleeping Tigers," in ibid.

12. Ratti and Westbrook, 1973: 157.

Any group thought potentially troubling to the new regime was quickly and brutally suppressed. Some such groups survived by kowtowing to the Tokugawa, others survived by adapting. For example, some *Otokodata* ("specialized fighting groups") survived to become *Yakuza* (the so-called Japanese "Mafia"). Other fighting cadre, Samurai and *Ninja* alike, took the opposite option, joining the growing Imperial Police Force.

This was a trying, transitional period with some Samurai trying desperately to preserve the ideal of Samurai, while facing a rapidly changing reality where the ability to tally sums was increasingly valued over one's ability to wield a sword:

> It must be explained that in those days foul play equaled strategy. —U. A. Casal[13]

All these lineages—martial arts schools (overt and covert), clandestine cadre and secretive societies (some working for the status quo, some against), and nascent medieval Japanese business interests—all hold Miyamoto Musashi in high regard. Indeed, in one way or another—true, deliberately falsified, or else fanciful—all trace themselves, if not physically, then philosophically, back to Kensei.

Thus, in Japan today, on one side of Tokyo you'll find competing schools of *Kenjutsu,* each of which traces itself in an "unbroken lineage" back to Musashi. While on the other side of town, you'll find Japanese businessmen attending a strategy seminar where Musashi's *Gorin no sho* forms the basis for their hostile takeover of a rival corporation.

---

13. "The Lore of the Japanese Fan," *Monuments Nipponics* (Vol. 16, 1960).

HOW TWO SWORDS BECAME
THREE DIAMONDS

*"There is nothing more difficult to take in hand, more
perilous to conduct, or more uncertain to its success, than to
take the lead in the introduction of a new order of things."*
—*Niccòlo Machiavelli,* **The Prince,** *1513*

The *Shinobi Ninja* of central Japan had (have?) a saying: "There are
no new answers, only new questions." Simply put, people change little
down through the ages (sorry, Mr. Darwin), remaining susceptible to
the same hates and fears, lusts and ambitions as their forefathers. As a
result, it should come as no surprise (you were right, Mr. Santayana),
human history *does* tend to repeat itself.

Hold on. There's at least a little *good* news, too.

Musashi was right, right in all his observations of all the failings
and foibles of his fellow man, as well as his subsequent strategies to
elude, else exploit, those same faults.

Strategies that *still work today.*

And, yes, that is why we spend our time studying the Masters of
Old: Sun Tzu, Cao Cao, Hannibal, and Musashi.

We learn from the past so we can rule our future . . . and anyone
else's future foolish enough to get in our way!

Ever heard of Yataro Iwasaki? Bet you've heard of "Mitsubishi,"
huh?

In 1879, *Samurai* Yataro Iwasaki founded the Mitsubishi Corporation. *Mitsubishi* means "Three Diamonds"[14] in Japanese.

Before founding his company, Iwasaki wrote nine "Guiding Principles" both he and his employees pledged themselves to observe.
Adhering to these nine principles, Iwasaki's company not only sur-

---

14. Curiously, there was once a medieval *Ninja ryu*, whose symbol was the sign of "three
diamonds" . . . carved into their victims. See Lung and Tucker's *Nine Halls of Death* (Citadel
Press, 2007).

vived, but prospered down through to the modern day: building civilian vehicles during peacetime, converting to the manufacture of war materials during both WWI and WWII (when they made engines for the infamous "Zero" fighter planes). Today, of course, Mitsubishi remains at the forefront of the world's automotive industry.

All who know of him agree Iwasaki possessed rare insight into human nature. Rare insight into human nature he learned from Musashi?

Musashi was, at the very least, an influential contributor to Iwasaki's overall philosophy and a close examination of Iwasaki's nine principles shows them to be, if not borrowed freely from, then surely in sync with, Musashi's own.

Like Musashi's, Iwaski's principles have stood the test of time, both being easily applicable to our own troubled times.

THE NINE PRINCIPLES OF IWASAKI

I. Do not be preoccupied with small matters but aim at the management of large enterprises.

Think big . . . and then do big. Note that Iwasaki does not say we should *ignore* "small matters," causing us to squander our resources on trivial concerns.

Of course Sun Tzu would tell us that if we develop the capacity to perceive "small problems" *before* they have a chance to become "big problems," then we've already won the battle.

In the West they tell you, "Don't sweat the small stuff," forgetting to add that, if you spy a problem early enough, "It's *all* small stuff!"

> Strategy is the science of making use of space and time.
> I am more jealous of the latter than of the former.
> We can always recover lost ground, but never lost time.
> —Field Marshal August von Gneisenau (1761–1831)[15]

---

15. See *The Art of Modern War*, Hermann Foetsch (1940).

According to Musashi:

> If you do not look at things on a large scale it will be dif-
> ficult for you to master strategy.

Musashi called this "rat's head, ox head." Simply put: don't miss the forest for the trees. It's important to draw a balance between the two, between concentrating too much on small details (the skunk smelling only his own tail, if you will) to the point where we fail to see where our little world fits into a whole larger world of goings-on, aka "the Big Picture."

Brutal example? A farmer in Idaho grows the best potato crop in the country and readies to truck his crop to market. However, he's failed to monitor "the Big Picture" and thus hasn't heard about the new deal D.C. just made to buy potatoes from some backwater Third World nation. Needless to say, Mr. Idaho Potato Farmer is gonna be disappointed with the low price (if any) he's offered for his crop at market this year.

Even more brutal example? At the beginning of World War II, Poland had the finest cavalry in Europe, having spent a ton of money and countless man hours training this elite horse-mounted force second-to-none. . . . Did you catch the "beginning of World War II" part? Hitler told 'em, "Tanks for the memories!"

Thus in the "Wind" section of his *Gorin no sho*, Musashi tells us:

> The spirit of my school is to win through the wisdom of
> strategy, paying no attention to trifles.

Yes, this does seem to contradict his advice in the "Ground" section:

> Pay attention even to trifles.

But obviously what he's teaching us is not to allow ourselves to be distracted, disturbed, or dissuaded by *superfluous* information. Having sifted through all incoming intelligence flotsam and jetsam, we now free up our mental resources for concentration on "the Big Picture."

II. Once you start an enterprise, be sure to succeed in it.

Finish the job or the job will finish you. You never *start* writing a novel unless you know how the story's gonna *end*. There's always leeway to change elements of the story, perhaps even altering your original ending—finding a way to leave an especially good originally *doomed* character alive at the end, for example. But you never press that first key until you have a plausible ending.

In the same way, you never initiate an endeavor without some *realistic* idea of how the venture will end.

The axiom that "no battle plan survives first contact with the enemy" is literally carved in stone worldwide . . . on millions of *cemetery headstones!*

> The merit of action lies in finishing it to the end.
> —Genghis Khan (1162–1227)[16]

III. Do not engage in speculative enterprises.

> *"Never strike a King unless you're certain you can kill him."*
> —Ancient Chinese adage

Get the facts and then act on those facts. Strike only when certain. What's that about "a bird in the hand being worth two in the bush"? (What? You thought our Eastern brothers were the only ones who could come up with really "deep" sayings? Heh-heh-heh.)

Bottom line? Any bomb-disposal expert will assure you, "It's always better to know which wire to cut." *Guess* . . . and you wind up with a *mess!*

---

16. Quoted in Tsouras (2005), 325.

IV. Operate all enterprises with the national interest in mind.

It's not possible to live, let alone operate a business, in a vacuum. Especially in today's world, *everything is connected*. No, you *don't* have to "like it," but you'd be a fool not to at least acknowledge the fact that your safety and prosperity, along with that of your loved ones, is intricately connected to what the dumb-ass next door and that loose cannon down the street are up to. And it doesn't matter if "the dumb-ass next door" and/or that "loose cannon" just happen to live in some country on the other side of the globe. When they finally get around to blowing each other up (hold the applause), unfortunately they'll probably take the rest of us along with them. So yeah, like it or not, we *do* have to "give a rat's ass."

The positive spin on all this: the more we expand our own enterprises outward, the better the chances we'll discover new resources and revenue, new "partners-in-crime" who can help us prosper even more. They, in turn, will see the wisdom of working *with* us rather than plotting *against* us . . . or else. It's called "reciprocity." Look it up.

Iwasaki's "national interest" in this instance refers back to "the Big Picture" we were just talking about. This is also what Musashi is talking about when he tells us to "Taste the Wind," i.e., make sure we align our interests with those of the Powers-That-Be . . . else we must cleverly hide our true agenda *very well* from the Powers-That-Be.

V. Never forget the pure spirit of public service and sincerity.

"Sincerity" here is translated from the Japanese *makoto*, whose meaning is "Do what you say, say what you do."

"Mr. Community Service" probably doesn't immediately spring to mind when searching for synonyms for "Miyamoto Musashi." Yet despite his (literally!) unwashed years spent wandering, seemingly a social pariah, by the time he got around to writing *Gorin no sho*, an older, wiser Musashi had learned enough to include "public justice" (as close to "public service" as we're likely to get with Musashi) in his list of virtues (and responsibilities) worth cultivating:

> You must cultivate your wisdom and spirit. Polish your wisdom: learn public justice, distinguish between good and evil, study the Ways[17] of different arts one by one.

For Iwasaki and Mitsubishi, especially when just starting out in business, it was vital to consider "the Big Picture" of national interests, if only for knowing what to invest in (i.e., peacetime vehicles versus war machines?). But Iwasaki also needed to cultivate good community relations: playing politics with the "macrocosm" of national and international movers and shakers (i.e., "Taste the Wind, Ride the Wave"), while also cultivating "sincere" community relations at the local microcosm level (the well from whence he would draw his men and raw materials).

Deal honestly and up front (*makoto*) and your detractors will have to scavenge further and further afield to find a stick with which to beat you.

VI. Be hardworking, frugal, and thoughtful to others.

"Hold on with a bulldog grip, and chew and choke as much as possible."
—*Lincoln's advice to Grant, 1864*

You can set the bar high . . . or you can sit in a bar high. Which one do you think's gonna get the job done?

Iwasaki gives us three practical virtues that, if we do not already

---

17. I.e., *do*, method and path.

possess, then we must make diligent effort to either acquire them sincerely, else feign them convincingly! They are:

- Be hardworking;
- Be frugal; and
- Be thoughtful of others.

Another word for "hardworking" in China is *kung-fu*.[18]

Hand-in-hand with being "hardworking" is using our tools and resources wisely; that's called being "frugal." "Waste not, want not." (Told you we in the West can go toe-to-toe when it comes to spouting out useful philosophical zingers!)

As for being "thoughtful of others"? Just good common sense.

As already mentioned, like it or not Mr. Unabomber, both our safety and our prosperity often depend on the kindness of strangers. Or, to be more accurate, on the *self-interest* of others.

In case you're new to the whacky world of Dr. Lung thinking: There's no such thing as "altruism." Even the proverbial "Good Samaritan" got paid, if only in bolstering his own feeling of self-worth in thinking himself doing what a "good person" should do.

Others? *Non*-Good Samaritans? You can almost always get their attention by blatantly waving around a Franklin, explaining "what's in it for them."

Far from being cynical, this actually leans more toward being optimistic, as in: if you take the time to show people "what's in it for them," then they'll throw their lot in with you.

For some the "bribery"[19] tipping point might be that Franklin you're waving around. For others, it'll be helping all the starving little children in South Turdistan.

That we all *have* a tipping point isn't in question, but *where* on the

---

18. Also spelled *gung-fu*.
19. "Bribery," one of those tried-'n'-true "6 Killer B's."

slippery, sliding scale of human morality our personal tipping point is to be found?

And, since people are pretty much selfish, hairless little monkeys (if not through evolution then simply by way of laziness!), and since "monkey see, monkey do," maybe, just maybe, if people see *you* being "thoughtful" of them . . . there's a chance, they may *reciprocate*.[20]

VII. Utilize proper personnel.

Ancient strategists, from Sun Tzu to Ssu-ma,[21] Hannibal to Patton, all able commanders know how the course of a major war can hinge on the outcome of a single battle, which, in turn, is often dependent on that commander's decision of *how quickly* to put *how many* boots *where* on the ground.

On the domestic side, if you allow your harping wife to kvetch you into hiring her lay-about brother, don't look surprised when your bottom line takes a kick in the crotch!

Likewise, *breasts* don't type.

In many ways, putting the right person in the right position at the right time, whether the right general on the right battlefield at the right time, the right CEO in the right negotiating room at the right time, or the right lover in *your* bedroom at the right time—picking the "proper personnel" to get the job done right the first time, spells the difference between "sorry" and "success."

Napoleon was once asked, "Which are the best troops?" to which he responded, "Those that win battles."

---

20. Aren't you glad you took the time to look up "reciprocity" earlier? Heh-heh-heh.

21. For a complete rendering of the philosophy and practical strategy of Chinese master strategist T'an Jan-chu, aka Ssu-ma, see "The Slyness of Ssu-ma" in Lung and Prowant's *Mind Warrior: Strategies for Total Mental Domination* (Citadel Press, 2010).

VIII. Treat your employees well.

"Too quick to praise, too quick to punish
The first makes men love themselves too much.
The latter makes men hate Their Lord[22] too much.
No matter. I know the uses of hate."
—The Answers of Attila

Take care of your people and they'll take care of you.

All too often we've seen both politicians and pop stars blaze suddenly into the spotlight, only to later burn out simply for lack of censure and good advice. Example: Hitler.

Clawing his way to power surrounded by a familiar (if equally despicable) cohort, none of whom were afraid to challenge Ol' Adolf when they thought he was making a mistake and/or getting a little big for his britches. Unfortunately (so far as that whole "Thousand-Year Reich" thing went), the more power Hitler obtained, the further afield spread his inner circle, and the less *reality* Hitler was hearing (since he increasingly found himself surrounded by yes men and adoring lap dogs too terrified to give the almighty Fuhrer bad news). Lacking realistic real-time intelligence, Hitler was doomed.

So, too, Michael Jackson. Without a reliable "posse" to sober you up and kick your ass out onto that stage, more than one entertainer has gone down in flames. By choice and inclination, Michael Jackson became increasingly isolated and on his own. Thus, when shocking allegations were lobbed his way, he had no one in his "inner circle" who could swear on a stack of Korans, "No really, he was with me on the other side of Neverland when that little boy lost his Barney the Dinosaur underpants!"

Take care of your people and they'll take care of you. . . . Of course, if you don't have *any* people watching your back. . . . Don't be surprised when you end up on TMZ.

---

22. Some render this "me," with Attila referrring specifically to himself.

> *"Pay heed to nourishing the troops; do not unnecessarily*
> *fatigue them. Unite them in spirit; conserve their*
> *strength. . . . Thus, such troops need no encouragement to be*
> *vigilant. Without exhorting their support the general obtains*
> *it; without inviting their affection he gains it; without*
> *demanding their trust, he wins it."*
> —Sun Tzu

IX. Be bold in starting an enterprise but meticulous in its prosecution.

This is where both your *Sen-ki* "war spirit" and your *Taido* "fast draw" are put into play.

Having placed all your ducks in a row, having dotted every "I" and crossed every "T," plans and personnel in accord—*strike!*

Thus the martial arts adage:

In seeking, *know.* In knowing, *strike!* In striking, *strike well.*
And, in striking well, accomplish all things!

Recall, this is the same technique you learned in the our section on *Iaido-jutsu*:

* Your blade does not leave the scabbard until you strike.
* A single smooth telling strike does the job.
* And then, with follow-through and flourish, your sword leaps back into the scabbard.
* The enemy dies never having seen your blade leave the scabbard.

So, too, in our "oh-so-more civilized" times, your business or love rival never suspects you preparing to move against him.

Unexpectedly blindsided by your initial stroke, his only hope of survival is to frantically backpedal, staunch what hemorrhaging he can, and *flee* with what little of life and larder you've so graciously allowed him to keep.

"Chance favors the prepared mind," 'tis true enough. Now the rest of that winning formula: "The prepared mind rides to victory on the horned and hackled back of *boldness*."

In his *Ping-fa*, Sun Tzu warns that "success has never been associated with long delay."

While it's often true that "slow and steady *can* (and often does) win the race," it never hurts to leap from the starting gate like a hare with your cottontail on fire.

Do it now. Do it well. Do it right the first time. In this, where is there time for doubt, or room for failure?

In another time and place, the *ronin* Miyamoto Musashi might have offered his services to a *Daimyo* or even a *Shogun* named Yataro Iwasaki.

Another reality, and Musashi the *ronin* finds himself first fighting against, and then learning from, a *Ninja Jonin* of the feared *Twasaki-Ryu*.

Still another convergence of time and coalescence of place, and a young, bright-eyed, but humble would-be swordsman named Yataro endures weeks of rain and cold sitting outside the secluded cave of the mysterious Sword Master everyone calls *Kensai,* in the hopes he will be taken on as his student. . . .

But then, in this sorry excuse for a reality we call home, young Yataro Iwasaki *did* learn from Musashi—though Master and Student, *Kohei* and *sempei,* were separated by hundreds of years. And yet, even after achieving great success and wealth using the same principles Musashi had used to survive over sixty duels-to-the-death, till his dying day the elder Iwasaki's dog-eared copy of *Gorin no sho* was never out of reach.

How close is *your* copy?

V.

108 Secrets of the Samurai (and a Few New Tricks Even They Never Heard Of!)

PART OF TEACHING *NINJA* students to think on their feet was a mental and physical exercise requiring them to find at least *five* uses for any single object. This was/is not so difficult when you consider all the uses for, say, a rope. Or even a sword. For example, *Ninja ninpo* swords were notorious for both their multiple uses (e.g., as a climbing tool, strangling tool, etc.) and for the multitude of additional tools and weapons that could be hidden *within* such a sword.[1]

However, finding multiple applications for an object becomes increasingly difficult when trying to come up with "five" uses for more mundane, everyday objects.

Ah! But therein lies the genius of the *Ninja* method: on guard against some "new" technique, we fall to the oldest of tricks, and

---

1. For a complete training course in the ancient art of *Ninjutsu*, see Dr. Lung's *The Ninja Craft* (Alpha Publications of Ohio, 1997), as well as his Knights of Darkness (Citadel Press, 2007).

instead of being taken down by an esoteric new "*Ninja*" weapon, we are felled by some street punk's alley-apple!

Mentally, practicing seeing at least five uses for any object (and person?) keeps us ever alert for new opportunities, while guarding us against attack by new enemies using old tried-'n'-true tactics.

Physically, mastering at least five uses for everything (and everybody?) in our environment adds a myriad of new tools (people included!) to our defensive and offensive arsenal.

Musashi, Munenori, and other Samurai of similar bent and intent, also went out of their way to find new tactics and techniques hidden in "old," familiar tricks. This is how a martial art grows . . . and how warriors stay alive.

PREDATOR VERSUS PREY

- Prey attracts predators. Don't be prey.
- It is estimated that only 10 percent of all animals are pure predators, meaning that, while they prey on other animals, they themselves have no natural enemies preying on them.

If we extrapolate this out to human beings, that means that only 10 percent of us are natural-born predators, while the rest of you are prey. . . .

5 USES FOR STRAW

- Use for insulation; stuff it and other such stuffing (e.g., newspaper) under your clothing to keep warm in a survival situation.
- Straw can be used as a fuel source for starting a fire.
- At night, stuffing straw and other materials under your clothing helps distort and disguise your natural silhouette (i.e., to make you look larger), helping throw off pursuers.
- *Amettori-jutsu* (Jp. "man of straw") is a *Ninja* ploy where a dummy silhouette is set up to trick your enemies as to (1)

where you are, and/or (2) how many sentry you have guarding a particular spot. In the West this ploy is known as *The Beau Geste*.

- In espionage-speak, a "straw man" (sometimes called a "cutout") is a proxy (or "patsy") you set up to take the blame so you and/or your more valuable agents can escape detection. Does the name "Lee Harvey Oswald"[2] ring a bell?

4 WAYS TO MAKE PEOPLE LIKE YOU

If people like you they are less likely to be suspicious of you, huh?

- *People like people who are like them.*
- *People like people who like them.*
- *People like people who cater to their "Sensory Modes"*: People are either "Watchers" (processing the world through what they see), "Listeners" (taking in most of their information through their ears), or "Touchers" (interacting with the world primarily through the senses of touch and taste). By observing and listening to a person you can quickly identify their "sensory modality," then adjust your speech and actions to better "accommodate" them.[3]
- *Mirror the other person's actions.* To the best of your ability *without* appearing to mock the other person, *imitate their* speech and body mannerisms. Remember: We like people who are *like* us.

---

2. See "Oswald and the Sleeping Tiger" in Dr. Lung's *Mind Penetration* (Citadel Press, 2007).

3. For a complete course on learning to recognize and manipulate another person's sensory modality, see "Verbal Phrases That Betray Us" in Lung and Prowant's *Mental Dominance* (Citadel Press, 2009).

4 WAYS TO WIN PEOPLE OVER

- People love to hear their own names.
- Upon being introduced to someone, always repeat their name. (1) This flatters them, and (2) repeating their name helps you remember that name.
- Always include the word "because" when asking someone to do something for you.
- Always tell the person what's in it for them. There's no such thing as "altruism," but even saints like to be tempted from time to time just to prove to everyone else (and themselves?) "how strong" they are.

5 THINGS THAT TEMPT PEOPLE THE MOST

"I can resist anything but temptation."
—*Oscar Wilde*

Here are the five things that tempt people the most:[4]

	Men	Women
Sex	50%	22%
Food	29%	56%
Money	14%	15%
Alcohol	7%	2%
Power	2%	7%

3 TYPES OF "SHIT"

According to Fritz Perls (1893–1970), founder of the *Gestalt* school of psychology, there are three kinds of verbal "shit" we are confronted with when talking to people:

- *Chicken shit* is small talk, devoid of any emotional content or commitment. If you catch someone talking chicken shit, they

---

4. See *USA Today*, March 9, 2001.

are (1) bored, and simply "passing time," or else (2) they are hiding something by avoiding talking about it. Con men use chicken shit (aka "smalltalk") to distract (and you can, too).

• *Bullshit* is exaggeration designed to (1) conceal truth, and (2) puff up one's importance.

• *Elephant shit* includes all the grandiose plans of what a person is going to do when they win the lottery or when the Universe finally gets around to recognizing their "natural genius." Like chicken shit, elephant shit is devoid of any actual commitment since the person doing the talking never has to actually "put up or shut up"—since there's not much chance of him ever actually winning the lottery. And that whole "the Universe finally recognizing his natural genius" thing? Yeah . . . Not holding out a lotta hope for that ever happenin', either!

3 WAYS TO TELL WHAT PEOPLE REALLY THINK OF YOU

• *We take correction from our Superiors.* If the person keeps trying to "correct" you, they *think* they're your "superior." If you're their boss and they resist *your* attempts to correct them, they do not respect your authority. Invite them to a long walk on a short pier.

• *We argue with Equals.* If a subordinate constantly challenges you, their boss—beware!—they're after your job. Conversely, if you find yourself repeatedly arguing with your boss, then, at least subconsciously, you do not respect him in a position over you. Either (1) get another job, or else (2) stage a coup.

• *We lecture Subordinates.* If someone "talks down" to you, they think they're better than you. Show them different. If you find yourself "talking down" to someone, then you (at least subconsciously) "suspect" you're superior to them. . . . Nietzsche would be proud.

5 RULES FOR LYING SUCCESSFULLY[5]

- *Lie only as a last resort.*
- *Don't lie on the telephone.* It's easier for the person at the other end to pick up on hesitations and trembles in your voice. If you have to lie over the telephone, place a mirror in front of you to provide you with feedback.
- *Watch your natural body language.* Beware of "micro-expressions" and other body tics and twitches that betray the fact that you're lying.
- *Insert deliberately deceptive body language.* Poker players often deliberately give off false "tells" designed to (1) disguise any true tells they might subconsciously display, and (2) mislead their opponents into betting big since they (think they) can read you like a book. Right! The maverick version of "When strong, appear weak." A simpler version of deliberately falsifying your body language is the way you do that oh-so-cute smile and slightly lower your head—pretending to be shy—in order to score with the babes.
- *Practice, practice, practice!* Like anything else, lying gets easier, and you (hopefully)get better at it the more you do it.

10 COMMANDMENTS FOR LYING SUCCESSFULLY

- *Lie as little as possible.* The more banks you rob, the less your chances of getting away with it, huh?
- *Respect Nature and Number.* Keep your lies within the realm of possibility. In other words, *respect your audience.*
- *The devil is in the details.* Bad liars tend to be too vague. Add interesting and amusing details as a distraction.

---

5. See Suzette Haden Elgin, Ph.D. *Success with the Gentle Art of Verbal Self-Defense* (Prentice Hall, 1989).

- *The telling is in the telling.* Believe in your ability to successfully tell your lie and people will believe your lie.
- *Be hard on yourself.* Self-deprecating asides and humor likewise distract people. Too much overt bullshit (i.e., bragging on yourself) too soon stinks up the place.
- *Put your Ass into it.* Make sure your body language matches the lie you're telling.
- *Put your heart into it.* Emotion is the fuel for any good lie. Inject your own (feigned) emotion in order to engage their emotions. Life is the tall glass you can fill either with the cool, clear, refreshing water of reason, or else with a heady drunkard's portion of emotion.
- *Stick to your guns.* Pick a lie and stick to it. No switching horses in midstream.
- *Keep track of your lies.*
- *People believe what they want to believe.* (1) Find out what they *want* to believe. (2) Feed them a chicken shit/bullshit/elephant shit sandwich: your thin lie nestled in between two thick slices of what they want to believe. Hold the mayo.

6 WAYS TO ROCK YOUR ENEMY TO SLEEP

- Human beings are more lazy and less observant near the end of a work shift.
- Human beings are more lax after (1) smoking, (2) eating, and/or (3) having sex.
- Human beings become more lax and less observant the closer they get to home. This is why most auto accidents happen within a few miles of a person's home.
- Lying down reduces our sensitivity to both smells and sound.
- We can cause other people to yawn by yawning (or faking a yawn) ourselves. Musashi called this "Passing It On."
- Besides yawning, other things such as scratching and relaxing can also be "passed on" from one person to another, either

subconsciously or else deliberately, thanks to "mirror neurons" in our brains that mimic actions we see in others, as if we were the ones actually doing the thing.

10 WAYS WE ARE BETRAYED BY OUR BODIES

- Pupils make the best pupils. Wide eyes with large pupils betray interest. Why men love pornography. Mystery solved!
- Likewise, licking lips and rubbing hands together betray interest.
- Just before your enemy reaches for his chess piece (or his pistol!), ask him if he knows what a "spiral staircase" is. When asked to describe a spiral staircase, human beings inevitably circle their index finger in the air. Saying the words "spiral staircase" the instant before a person reaches to move a chess piece (or draw a weapon) causes their hand to hesitate in unconscious anticipation of having to make the "sign" in the air for *spiral staircase*.
- When searching, especially inside buildings, human beings seldom look up or down. This is called "line of sight." Thus, when sneaking up on a sentry, *Ninja* were (are) taught to come in low, under the targeted person's line of sight.[6]
- Fat sentries never squat down to look under beds or cars (parked, entering a compound, etc.),nor do they like climbing stairs to check in the attic, on the roof, etc. . . .
- When children run away they tend to run away *downhill*. Search for them downhill.
- Untrained escapees (e.g., POWs) naturally gravitate toward structures (e.g., houses, barns, bridges, etc.). Search for them there.

---

6. See Dr. Lung's *The Ancient Art of Strangulation* (Paladin Press, 1995), and *Knights of Darkness* (Citadel Press, 2004).

- People being chased veer left when coming to a "T" in the road, alley, etc.
- When trying to convince someone, move from your right to your left when emphasizing your point.
- In order to draw a person closer to you, after beginning at one volume of speech, lower your voice, making the listener lean in closer and/or step closer in order to continue hearing what you are saying.

THE 2 BRAINS
(AND HOW TO CONFUSE THEM BOTH!)

Despite being born left-handed, Miyamoto Musashi was able to use both sides of his body equally. This may have originally come from the fact that his father, like many parents still today, when confronted with a naturally left-handed child, may have forced his child to use his right hand, thinking to "deprogram" the child from using their left hand and thus grow up "normal."

Despite old wives' tales about how forcing a left-handed child to use his right hand will make that child grow up to be a stutterer, left-handed children forced at an early age to use their right hands often simply grow up ambidextrous, as was probably the case with Musashi.

As with the rest of the body, the more you know about how the human *brain* is put together, the easier it is to *take it apart*.

Thus:

- The human brain is actually *two* brains, a right, abstract-oriented hemisphere and a left, more concrete-oriented hemisphere.
- Each hemisphere controls the *opposite* side of the body.
- The right hemisphere is a *listener* while the left side is a *talker.*
- The "past" is on a person's left side, thus, when trying to convince a person of something stand close by the left ear.
- The "future" is on a person's right side. Thus, when attempt-

ing to sell a person on a novel idea or on something that will happen "in the future" (e.g., their getting rich by investing in one of your schemes), position yourself to talk into their right ear.

- When trying to talk yourself out of a physical confrontation, slowly circle left so as to position yourself more on your opponent's right side as you explain how the future is not going to be bright if your opponent carries through his intent to attack you.
- When trying to convince them to "go forward" with an idea, physically walk them forward(e.g., toward the car you want them to buy).
- When attempting to evoke past experiences, have the person sit down, or else gently lead them *back* into an area where you've both already been.

THE 2 BRAINS
(AND HOW TO USE THEM BOTH!)

Want to double your brain capacity by learning to *consciously* use both sides of your brain?

- Learn to draw. See *Drawing on the Right Side of the Brain* by Betty Edwards.
- Listen to music without lyrics (words being a left side operation, remember?).
- Meditate. A common practice of meditation is stopping the "internal dialogue human beings constantly maintain with themselves," that is, in effect, the left-verbal side of your brain talking to the more taciturn right side. Too much of this "internal dialogue" prevents us from hearing what's happening "outside." Skunk smelling his own ass again.
- If you're naturally right-handed, try brushing your teeth, writing, and doing other activities with your left hand.

- Talk to your brain. If right-handed, take a pencil and write "What's happening?" Then switch the pen to your left hand and *quickly* write (or draw) whatever you're thinking.
- Write backward. Anytime a right-handed person draws a line (let alone tries to write "backward" from right to left), they automatically kick their right hemisphere into action.
- While sitting watching TV, place a pen and pad in your left hand (your right hand, if already left-handed). Allow your left hand to "doodle" while you're watching TV. Later, study these right-side doodlings with your conscious left-side focus.
- Martial arts students, after "mastering" a set of formalized *kata* moves, then go on to learn the same *kata* on the opposite side of their body. Often performing a *kata* "mirror" reveals new applications for a *kata* that has become routine.
- In ancient times, Chinese martial arts masters often "disguised" their fighting styles by making new students learn the fighting forms *in reverse,* only later to be shown the (literally) right way to do the form. Recall that tradition has Bodhidharma first teaching the brothers of Shaolin "peaceful" meditation exercises designed to help them stay awake during the marathon meditation sessions he demanded of them. Only later would he reveal to the brethren the "hidden" martial-arts applications of those same "meditation" exercises.
- Literally *beat someone with one hand tied behind your back.* A good training exercise for martial arts students is to literally tie one hand behind their back, forcing them to "step up" their blocking and kicking game by "deliberately" handicapping them. (1) Not only does it force the student to "break through" to the next level, but (2) it has the practical "street" application of teaching students to defend themselves even when they have a wounded arm.
- *Hoodwinking* or otherwise blindfolding a student is another way of making them "kick in" their right hemisphere (since this side is a "listener," important when you can't see, and is

responsible for our spatial sense, important for maintaining balance.

- Each brain hemisphere has its own, easily discernible traits.

5 USES FOR RICE

- The sixteenth-century Samurai Kamiizimi Midetsuna tossed a rice cake to an enraged man who was holding a child hostage. Instinctively the crazed man let go of the child as he reached to catch the flying rice cake. At that instant, Kamiizumi seized hold of the man's extended arm, subduing him with a *jui-jutsu* hold.
- Samurai *Daimyo* would often sprinkle rice outside their sleeping quarters, rice that crackled loudly underfoot anytime an intruder tried creeping near. When breaking and entering by stealth, *Ninja* would likewise sprinkle rice behind them to alert them to anyone's approach. A modern-day variation of this has a burglar stuffing toothpicks into the front door, so as to alert the burglar to the untimely return of the house's rightful occupants.
- Ancient Chinese magistrates often forced witnesses to eat a mouthful of rice powder, the theory being that a lying man's mouth would already be dry and, with the introduction of the rice powder, he would be unable to speak (let alone tell further lies).
- Rice (or any other such substance, the more toxic the better!) can be dashed into an attacker's eyes to both blind them and choke their nostrils and throat. In a kill-or-be-killed street fight, the rule is that any time your hand touches the ground (e.g., when you're knocked to the ground or when you drop to the ground in order to defend yourself with your legs), you should fill your hand (with dirt, sand, sticks and stones).[7]

---

7. For a complete self-defense course incorporating such *realistic* street fighting common sense, see Dr. Lung's *Mind Fist: The Asian Art of the Ninja Masters* (Citadel Press, 2008).

- Of course, rice is also an easily carried food source, especially for a group of fast-moving medieval *Ninja*.

7 USES FOR A SMALL MIRROR

- A small handheld mirror is useful when putting on an impromptu disguise.[8]
- Use a small mirror (or any available reflective surface) to signal cohorts and/or to call attention to your position when in need of rescue.
- Dangle a mirror (or other small reflective surface) from a tree limb (where it is sure to be jostled by the winds, creating flashes) in order to deliberately draw a curious enemy away from your true path of escape and/or draw them into ambush.
- Use a mirror (or other reflected surface, e.g., a sword blade) to temporarily blind an enemy, shining it always behind your own back and in your enemy's eyes. The reason being, at least in fictional accounts, as to why gunfighters were always scheduled at "High Noon," when the sun was directly over *both* gun-fighters' heads.
- When you suspect you're being followed, use a small compact mirror, mirrors of nearby autos, or any other such reflecting surface to spot whoever is "tailing" you.[9]
- Mirrors can also be broken and the shards used as weapons.[10]
- See "Five Rules for Lying Successfully."

---

8. See "The Sixth Hall: The Art of Disguise" in Lung and Tucker's *The Nine Halls of Death: Ninja Secrets of Mind Mastery* (Citadel Press, 2007).

9. For a complete training course in the art of surveillance, see Dr. Lung's *Knights of Darkness: Secret Fighting Techniques of the World's Deadliest Night-Fighters* (Citadel Press, 2004).

10. For a complete training course on the use (and abuse) of such "Environmental Weapons," see *Death on Your Doorstep: 101 Weapons in the Home* by Ralf Dean Omar (Alpha, 1984).

4 WAYS TO TRAIN DOGS . . . AND PEOPLE TOO!

- *Inu Kuguri No Ho*: Obtaining knowledge of the instincts and habits of dogs[11] in general and specific breeds in particular helps you target and train dogs (and people) to tricks and tasks they are best suited to (e.g., guard dogs, as opposed to poodles). Study your target, learn his (or her) ways: likes and dislikes, hobbies, friends, and family. What are their personal, social, religious, and political "triggers"? What "treats" can you bribe them with to perform the tricks you want them to perform?

- *Gukenjutsu*: Get a suspicious or "mean" dog comfortable with your "scent" by offering him/her treats and toys. For human "dog" targets, work your way into your target's confidence by way of his friends and family via "Six Degrees of Separation" ploys.[12]

- *Goken no ho* (literally, "distract a dog by using a dog of the opposite sex"): Lust is one of the perennial, tried-'n'-true "5 Warning F.L.A.G.S.," weaknesses all people are susceptible to, to varying degrees, in various combinations: Fear, Lust, Anger, Greed, and Sympathy. From the *Kama Sutra* to *Ninja kuniochi*,[13] if not sex then the lack of sex has brought down empires, *Shoguns*, and even a couple of presidents, as well.[14]

- *Kiai-jutsu*: For a dog, especially young pups about to transgress or trespass, a sudden sharp noise will frighten the dog into "shying" away from said trespass in the future. Martial artists and other warriors often use a "war-cry" (*kiai*) to (1) startle the enemy, and (2) "tighten" themselves, both mentally (focusing) and physically (tightening the abdomen) in preparation for

---

11. Simply exchange "people" for "dogs" when reading this!

12. See Lung and Prowant's *Black Science* (Paladin Press, 2001), and *Mind Manipulation* (Citadel Press, 2002).

13. *Ninja* female operative.

14. For more than you'll ever need to know on the art of *Sexual Feng Shui*, see Lung and Prowant's *Mental Dominance* (Citadel Press, 2009).

striking. "Classical conditioning" ring a bell? Right! The old "Pavlov rings a bell, dog gets reward" setup. Before long, the dogs salivate every time they hear the bell. FYI: This is also one way human beings develop "phobias" *and* fetishes. Zen Buddhism has also been accused of using this "whack-a-mole" method of training to shock its students into "enlightenment."

THE USES OF PATIENCE

Patience isn't only a "virtue." . . . It's also a *weapon*! Cases in point: The 47 Ronin, and the diminutive *Ninja* who spent days hiding under warlord Uesugi Kenshin's toilet in order to skewer him the minute he finally squatted.[15]

HOW TO OVERCOME FEAR

Ichi dai ji (pronounced "Itch-ee-die-gee") is a Buddhist chant meaning "This is unique." All too often, when facing an enemy or other stressful situation, we start rerunning negative brain-loops of past failures with *similar* content. "Ichi daji" is an affirmation that, *no matter how similar a situation first appears*, no matter how much it reminds you of a past incident where you failed or otherwise came up short, *this incident is unique*, allowing you to call new energies and possible new solutions into play.

THE 1-2-3 ATTACK RULE

- When using any attack, whether a physical martial arts attack or an attack directed at your enemy's psyche, strike once, then twice, *using the same or similar attack*. Then, *completely change up your third strike*, catching your opponent off guard. For example, a typical martial arts "attack run" would be punch-punch-

---

15. Adds a whole new meaning to "Stickin' it to da man!"

kick, or else kick-kick-punch. For some reason (as yet unknown), human beings *worldwide* like things in "3"s. Give them "1" and "2" and they will naturally fill in the blank with "3."

- **The same 1-2-3 rule applies to telling lies:** Tell two initial *true* statements, followed by your lie.

6 MEDITATION AND VISUALIZATION EXERCISES

- **The Flower Breathing Meditation** is accomplished by (1) seating yourself comfortably, then breathing in slowly and deeply as if you were smelling a big beautiful rose, as if trying to take in as much of the smell of that rose as possible. FYI: Don't be surprised if, after doing this "flower breathing" for a few minutes, you actually perceive the scent of a real rose.

- **Zen Counting Meditation** is accomplished by first seating yourself comfortably, then closing your eyes and breathing in a deep, slow breath while *mentally* intoning the letter "Z." Now exhale to "E." Again inhale to "N," and then exhale a second time to the number "1." Repeat this Z-E-N[16] breathing in and out, adding "2," "3," and then "4" with each repetition. Upon reaching "4," return to "1."

- **Navel Breathing** is accomplished by (1) first *visualizing* breathing in through your navel. Sure, we all know it's not physiologically possible to actually "breathe in" through your belly button. The purpose of this meditation exercise is that, when you think about breathing in through your navel, you *unconsciously* take in deeper breaths (drawing the breath in your lungs deeper, down toward your navel). Having drawn in a deep

---

16. When mentally intoning "Z," think about relaxing and "catching some Zs" (i.e., sleep). With "E," think "exhale." And with "N," see it as "Z" lying (comfortably and relaxed) on its side.

"navel" breath, slowly "push" your breath out through your nose, completely (but don't strain), before your next breath.

- **The Battle Breathing Meditation.** When facing a serious threat to your physical and/or mental equilibrium, draw in a slow and even breath while mentally counting off "B-R-E-A-T-H." The slower you draw in this breath, the more beneficial. Having drawn in a full breath through your nostrils, now slowly, but *forcefully*, exhale all the breath in your lungs out through your mouth to the mental intoning of "EEEEE." If you wish, you can even verbally express this "long e" sound. As you forcefully exhale, completing the word "B-R-E-A-T-H," you will notice a tightening of your abdomen. As this happens, mentally take note of the area three inches below your belly button. This is your *hara*, which Samurai regarded as both the seat of the soul and the reservoir of *ki*. If possible, press gently but firmly on your *hara* as you exhale.

- **The Go-ju Visualization** requires you keep a solid, hard object (e.g., small rock, pocket knife) in one pants pocket, while keeping a soft, squeezable object (e.g., ball of soft wax) in the opposite side pocket. When needing to relax, squeeze the soft object several times. Conversely, when you need to focus and/or are in need of a short burst of energy, seize hold of the hard object in your pocket for at least thirty seconds.

- **Visualize the outcome** of any situation as often and for as long as you can prior to the actual test, confrontation, job interview, *katana* sword duel to the death, etc. The human brain does not distinguish between something we actually experience and something we "imagine" or visualize. Therefore, by "seeing" in your "mind's eye" the outcome you want to experience, you help your mind "dig ditches" toward that outcome, "ditches" down which, when the time of testing actually arrives, your will and determination will easily "flow" toward—your visualized outcome.

HOW TO SPEAK TO A LARGE AUDIENCE

When experiencing anxiety at the prospect of having to give a speech before a large assembly, we're often given the advice to "just imagine your audience *naked*." No! Just *imagine yourself giving the speech naked* . . . and imagine your audience being *really impressed*.

SUN TZU'S 7 MOST IMPORTANT LESSONS

- *When strong, appear weak.* It makes people *underestimate* you.
- *Always leave your enemy a way out.* Men with no "opt out" clause have nothing to lose and so they fight tooth-'n'-nail till the end.
- *There are some battles not to be fought.*
- *Never move upstream to meet the enemy.* In other words, go with the flow, not against it.
- *Don't take the enemy's offers.*
- *Use spies.* But never trust them.
- *Know yourself. Know your enemy. Know your environment.* And in a hundred battles, you will never be defeated.

CONCLUSION

"A Good Sword Cuts Both Ways"

IN MEDIEVAL JAPAN, and still today, *Hin-ken* are highly prized . . . despite the inherent danger.

Hin-ken are swords that bring a person great wealth and power . . . but at a price.

For example, Samurai blades crafted by the great Senzo Muramasa (died 1341) are considered unstoppable, capable of bringing a warrior great victory and power. The downside is that Muramasa himself was a man prone to rage, and so, it's believed, his anger seeped into and saturated his magnificent, unbeatable blades.

Thus, anyone brave enough to wield a Muramasa blade runs the risk of being overcome (or "overshadowed," if you will) by the angry, malignant spirit (*oni*) that dwells within that blade. Daring to wield a Muramasa blade in combat, a weak-minded man might suddenly find himself thrown into uncontrollable, berserker[1] rage, and, in his blood lust, slaughter friend and foe alike.

---

1. From the Old Norse *berserkr* (*bjorn* meaning "bear" and *serkr* meaning "shirt"), fierce, enraged, unstoppable, and uncontrollable Viking warriors.

Thus, a Muramasa blade, like all blades, is capable of both gifting or gutting a friend or foe, depending on the hand that wields it.

The hand controls the sword. The mind controls the hand.

And of all swords, Musashi's *Mind-Sword* remains ever the most dangerous.

Properly cared for, diligently honed, it can instantly leap from its scabbard to defend kiln, kith, and kin.

Conversely, left to rust, left hanging too long on the wall, why are we surprised when our Mind-Sword sticks in its dusty scabbard, choking at the moment we need it the most?

Any weapon, no matter how advanced, can be stolen from you, whether a switchblade wrenched from your grip during an alley fight, or nuclear secrets spirited away via flash drive.

Even our Mind-Sword can be slowed, soiled, even broken by a thousand ancient and modern plots and ploys and computer programs of confusion, hypnotism, and brainwashing.

When the mind is lost, all is lost.

To their credit, some do prudently protect their mind against influence, against unwanted intrusion, and against theft. Some do this as practical precaution, others from deep paranoia, both burying their thoughts and memories beneath increasing layers of lock and key, in the hopes of some friendlier future. . . .

Ah, but there are others, a scant and sometimes scandalous sort, who daily test and temper and then test again the blade of their mind, regularly anointing that Mind-Sword with ever fresh oils, making ever keen the edge that promises them "the Edge" over their enemies.

Still, we're repeatedly warned, most often by those too fearful to ever take up the sword themselves, that "those who live by the sword, die by the sword!"

Too much history to deny.

Yet, when it comes to willfully wielding our Mind-Sword . . .

Better to *live* by the sword . . .
And let our enemies *die* by that same sword!

"These three things you must always keep in mind:
concentration of strength, activity, and a firm resolve to
perish gloriously."
—Napoleon

GLOSSARY

Amettori-jutsu: (Jp., lit. "a man of straw"). Encompasses all tactics and techniques of deception. The name comes from the ploy of dressing up a scarecrow to make an enemy think it is a real sentry or soldier.

ASP: "Additional Sensory Perception." The full use of our five senses that gives the impression to others we possess a "sixth sense," i.e., ESP.

Assassins: Medieval Muslim secret society noted for its terror, treachery, and mind-manipulation techniques.

Atari-kokoeo: Japanese mind-mastery techniques. (See *Kiai-shin-jutsu*.)

Autogenic: Self-generated therapies (e.g., biofeedback, self-hypnosis, meditation, auto-suggestion), coined by Zafutto and Zafutto, 1974.

Banking: Holding back valuable and/or damaging information (indiscretions, faux pas, etc.) you've discovered about a person for use in blackmailing and/or disgracing them at a later, more opportune time.

Big Brother: Oppressive government, always watching. Coined by George Orwell in his 1948 novel, *1984*.

Biometrics: System of scientific measurement of body parts and actions designed to give insight into intent. (See *Tells*.)

Bio-resources: People whose talents you can utilize to accomplish your goals.

Black Curtain, the: (Jp. *Kuromaku*, lit. "string-puller"). Generic, the veil of secrecy and skullduggery a sinister cadre hides behind. Synonym for "smoke screen." Specific, the head of a Japanese Yakuza crime family. (See *the Illuminati*.)

Black Science, the: Any strategy, tactic, or technique used to undermine a person's ability to reason and respond for themselves. Synonym for mind control and manipulation. First coined by researcher C. B. Black.

Blood ties: Dangerous and damaging information we hold over another. (See *the Killer B's*.)

C.H.A.O.S. Principle, the: "Create *Hazards* (Hurdles, Hardships, etc.) And Offer Solutions," i.e., profiting from difficulties and "crises" you have secretly created.

Cheng and Ch'i: (Ch.) "Direct" and "indirect" (i.e., sneaky) actions. Also spelled *Zhing* and *Qi*.

Cognitive dissonance: Mental anxiety created when a person must reconcile their contradictory ideas and/or actions.

Cult-speak: Special passwords and coded phrases cults and cliques use to identify one another while marginalizing "outsiders."

"Cutting-at-the-Edges": Principle coined by Miyamoto Musashi (1594–1645). When a powerful enemy cannot be attacked directly, undermine his confidence and ability to fight by attacking and otherwise eroding his "comfort zone" and support network (e.g., family, friends, and financial resources).

Dim-mak: (Ch.) Death touch.

"Dropping Lugs" (aka "Lyin' by Implyin'"): Using innuendo and rumor to plant doubt and seed suspicion, especially intended to undermine another's credibility.

Dyshemism: Words used as weapons. (See *Word Slavery*.)

Ekkyo: (Jp.) Divination methods that allow us to determine a victim's birth order and examine their interactions with others, especially close relatives.

ESP-ionage: Research and/or application of "Extra-Sensory Perception" to gather intelligence, e.g., when spying. (Aka Psi-War, not to be confused with PSYWAR, synonym for psychological warfare in general.)

Finders: The International Finders, European Freemason-esque secret society, linked to the *Illuminati*.

Five Warning F.L.A.G.S.: The five *Gojo-goyoku* weaknesses: Fear, Lust, Anger, Greed, and Sympathy.

Gojo-goyoku: (Jp.) "Five Element Theory." Derived from the Chinese pseudo-science of *wu-hsing*, which teaches that all reality (including actions and attitudes) is composed of five basic forces: earth, air, fire, water, and void. In all things and all times, one of these elements is dominant. Each element has a corresponding element in opposition to it. (See *Five Warning F.L.A.G.S.*)

Gray talk: Words and phrases deliberately crafted to confuse the listener.

Hyori: (Jp.) "Deception."

Illuminati, the: Generic, the ultimate secret society bugaboo and boogeyman. Whispered about for centuries, the *Illuminati* reportedly controls the world economy and pulls the "strings" of world politics from behind the "Black Curtain." Specific, secret society in Bavaria circa 1776.

In-yo-jutsu: (Jp.) Tactics designed to "unbalance" an opponent, to sow doubt and distrust in his mind.

Jodomon: (Jp., lit. "the way of the cat"). Individuals who take this approach depend on *tariki* ("another's power"). (See *Shodomon*.)

Jomon-jutsu: (Jp.) Use of special words and phrases designed to affect an individual's emotional stability, for example words evoking fear, lust, or patriotism.

Jujushin: (Jp.) Identifies "Ten Minds," or ten levels of understanding and functioning into which human beings can be categorized.

Junishi-do-jutsu: (Jp.) Employing the ancient art of Chinese astrology to determine a person's overall temperament as well as his weakest time of the day, when he is most susceptible to physical attack and mental manipulation.

Kami: (Jp.) Spirits, ghosts.

Kiai-shin-jutsu: (Jp.) Tactics and techniques that directly attack the intended victim psychologically by "shouting" into his mind. (See *Atari-kokoro*.)

Ki-dol: (Jp.) The ability to wield *ki* (Ch. *Ch'i*) force to influence and overpower another, e.g., especially through hypnosis.

Killer B's, the: Techniques for infiltrating an enemy's mind: Blind; Bribery and Blackmail; Blood ties; Brainwashing; Bully; and Bury.

Kuniochi: (Jp.) A female *Ninja*.

Kuroi-kiri: (Jp.) "The Black Mist," confusion in general.

Kuro-kakure: (Jp.) "Skullduggery," in general, a dark and hidden agenda.

Kuromaku: (Jp., lit. "a string-puller," originally from Kabuki.) A Yakuza chief. (See the *Black Curtain*.)

Kyonin-no-jutsu: (Jp.) Using an enemy's superstitions against him.

Makoto: (Jp., lit. "the stainless mind"). *Makoto* is a balanced state of mind allowing us to remain calm even in the most trying of circumstances. The development of *makoto* consists of the active cultivation and practice of two skills: *haragei* (awareness) and *rinkioken* (adaptability).

"Mama, Drama, and Trauma": Slang term for the "nurture" influences in a person's life (as opposed to the "nature" influences).

Masakatsu: (Jp., lit. "by any means necessary"). Strategy that allows for the use of any tactic or technique in order to achieve your goal, i.e., the end justifies the means.

Mekura: (Jp.) The "inner eye," i.e., insight and intuition.

Mind War: Preemptive measures (propaganda, etc.) used to attack an enemy's mind, intended to sap his will to fight before physical war becomes necessary. Sun Tzu's ideal.

MK: Spook-speak for "mind control." Coincidentally, these same initials are used to identify the Merck pharmaceutical company rumored responsible for helping government agencies develop "cogniceuticals." (See *Spook-speak*.)

Mushroom Treatment, the: Overall strategy for dealing with enemies (i.e., "Keep 'em in the dark and feed 'em plenty of bullshit!"), that is to deny them access to true information, while you feed them misinformation.

Ninja: (Jp., lit. "to steal in"). Assassin-spies (aka *Shinobi*) originating in medieval Japan, known for their stealth and skullduggery. Generic, anyone who employs stealth and secrecy to accomplish their ends.

One-eyed Snake: This strategy was comprised of tactics and techniques intended to give outsiders the illusion the *Ninja* possessed true magical powers, e.g., the power to strike down a foe from afar using ESP, kill with a single touch without so much as a mark left on the victim (*Dim mak*), and control others with mystical hypnosis. (See *Yugen-shin-jutsu*.)

Oni: Mythical demons of Japan. Shape-shifters that can range in size from miniature to gigantic. Often they act as evil spirits (*kami*), haunting people and places.

Pakua: (Ch.) The "Eight Trigrams," Pakua are eight symbols, consisting of three lines each. Each symbol represents one of eight basic relationships and interactions of life. Sometimes spelled *Baqua*.

Plausible deniability: Spook-speak for being somewhere else when the fecal matter collides with the oscillating rotor. (See *Spook-speak*.)

Propaganda: Rumor's big brother, or Big Brother's rumor.

"Propheteering": The Cult Game. Generic, hiding behind religion for deceitful and devious purposes.

Psychotronics: Any electronic device used to enhance or entrance the mind. In 1970s Czechoslovakia, *psychotronics* was used as a synonym for *parapsychology* (Ostrander and Schroeder, 1970).

Ronin: (Jp.) A masterless samurai. Generic: a rogue.

Satsujin: (1) (Jp., lit. "insight"). (See *Tells*.); (2) one of four divisions of Yakuza crime strategy meting out "murder."

Satsujin-jutsu: (Jp.) Insights into the minds or natures of men.

Seishinshugi: (Jp.) Literally "mind over matter."

Sennin: (Jp.) Master mind manipulators, "Mind Assassins."

Shadow-talk: Akin to Freudian slips. (See *Tells*.)

Shadow-walk: See *Tells*.

Shinjiraren!: (Jp., lit. "It boggles the mind!"). Exclamation used when amazed and/or confused by something. Generically, techniques designed to amaze and confuse.

Shodomon: (Jp., lit. "the way of the monkey"). Depends on *jiriki* ("one's own strength"). Individuals with this approach to life are independent; journeying alone, finding their own way; keeping their own counsel; and binding their own wounds, both physically and psychically. On the one extreme, these kinds of people are rugged individualists. At the opposite extreme, they are stubborn isolationists and control freaks, unable to take another's counsel. (See *Jodomon.*)

Siddhas: (Skt.) Enhanced powers of mind and body claimed by Hindu yoga mystics and *fakirs*. Sometimes used as the name for such masters themselves.

Sons of Brutus, the: Those elements (primarily people) left over after an operation (e.g., palace coup, hostile corporate takeover) that may prove "troubling" (i.e., seek revenge!) at some future date. According to the Romans (and Machiavelli), prudence calls for this element to be completely eliminated.

Spook-speak: Euphemism and code words used by intelligence agencies.

Suggestology: The science/art of suggestion. Includes and/or touches on hypnotism, the power of persuasion, propaganda, etc. Coined by Dr. Gregori Lozanov, Bulgaria. (See Ostrander and Schroeder, 1970.)

Tantric: (Skt., lit. "forbidden"). Taboo mystical practices (drugs, sex, necromancy, etc.) used by Hindu mystics as a shortcut to enlightenment and *siddhas*. Also spelled *Tantrik*.

Tells: Twitchin', itchin', and bitchin' body language and speech faux pas that inadvertently reveal what a person is really thinking and/or may reveal a person's unconscious desires and fears. Also known as "shadow-talk" and "shadow-walk."

Tengu: Mythical half-man, half-bird creatures from whom the *Ninja* claim descent. Tricksters.

Ten Minds, the: Buddhists use each of the "Ten Minds" (*jujushin*) as stepping-stones to enlightenment. For *Ninja*, on the other hand, the *jujushin* was just another block to place in the path of a foe. These Ten Minds are: Goat's Mind, Fool's Mind, Child's Mind, Dead Man's Mind, No-Karma Mind, Compassionate Mind, Unborn Mind, Single-Truth Mind, No-Self Mind, and Secret Mind. Each of the Ten Minds contains the seed of the others.

Thought Reform: Brainwashing by any other name.

Wa: (Jp.) Your spirit, presence, or intention.

Warning Flags, the: The five weaknesses: Fear, Lust, Anger, Greed, and Sympathy.

Word Slavery: The deliberate use of words and language to control and/or otherwise influence another human being. Includes the use of subliminals, culturally taboo words, slur words (insults) and purr words (lulling and soothing words).

Wu-hsing: (Ch.) "The Five Movers." This concept maintains that all reality is made up of five basic elements: earth (*chi*); air (*fu*); fire (*la*); water (*sui*); and void (*ku*).

Yakuza: Japanese "Mafia."

Yugen-shin-jutsu: (Jp., lit. "mysterious mind"). Uses various methods of hypnotism and subliminal suggestion to influence and control the minds of others.

Zen-zone: That level of functioning where stainless mental awareness (see *Makoto*) and physical awareness emerge, allowing us to instantly and effortlessly adapt to rapidly shifting circumstances.

Zetsutjin: (Jp., lit. "offspring of a talkative tongue"). An accomplished talker and manipulator, a mastermind.

Zhing and Qi: See *Cheng and Ch'i.*

SOURCES AND SUGGESTED READING

Baughman, Robert D. and Black, C. D. *666 Devilish Secrets of Islam*. Only Publications, 2010.

Bhagavad-Gita (The Song of God). Misc. translations.

Booking, Brian. *A Popular Dictionary of Shinto*. NTC Publishing Group, 1997.

Davis, Fei-Ling. *Primitive Revolutionaries of China*. University Press of Hawaii, 1971.

Deacon, Richard. *A History of the British Secret Service*. London, 1969.

De Mente, Boyé Lafayette. *Samurai Strategies: 42 Martial Secrets from Musashi's Book of Five Rings*. (Tuttle, 2005).

Dhammapada (Sayings of the Buddha). Misc. translations.

Draeger, Donn F. *Classical Buddhism*. Whitehall Press, 1973.

Elgin, Suzette Haden, Ph.D. *Success with the Gentle Art of Verbal Self-Defense*. Prentice Hall, 1989.

Herrigel, Eugen. *The Method of Zen*. Pantheon, 1960.

Kaplan, David E. and Dubro, Alec. *Yakuza*. Addison-Wesley Publishing Co., 1986.

Kosko, Bart. *Fuzzy Thinking: The New Science of Fuzzy Logic*. Hyperion, NY, 1993.

Krippendorf, Kaihan. *Hide a Dagger Behind a Smile*. AdamsMedia, 2008.

Lung, Dr. Haha, *The Ancient Art of Strangulation*. Paladin Press, 1995.

————. *Ninja Craft*. Alpha Publications of Ohio, 1997.

————. *Assassin! Secrets of the Cult of the Assassins*. Paladin Press, 1997.

————. *Knights of Darkness: Secrets of the World's Deadliest Night-Fighters*. Paladin Press, 1998.

————. *Cao Dai Kung-Fu*. Citadel Press, 2004.

————. *Assassin!* Citadel Press, 2004.

————. *Lost Fighting Arts of Vietnam*. Citadel Press, 2006.

————. *The 99 Truths: Hannibal's Black Art of War*. (Publication pending).

————. *666 Devilish Secrets of Lying*. (Publication pending).

————. *666 Devilish Secrets of Hypnosis*. (Publication pending).

Lung, Dr. Haha, and Prowant, Christopher B. *Black Science: Ancient and Modern-Day Techniques of Ninja Mind Manipulation*. Paladin Press, 2001.

————. *Shadowhand: Secrets of Ninja Taisavaki*. Paladin Press, 2002.

————. *Mind Manipulation*. Citadel Press, 2002.

————. *Theatre of Hell: Dr. Lung's Complete Guide to Torture*. Loompanics Unlimited, 2003.

————. *Ninja Shadowhand: The Art of Invisibility*. Citadel Press, 2004.

————. *Knights of Darkness*. Citadel Press, 2004.

————. *Mind Control*. Citadel Press, 2006.

————. *Mind Penetration*. Citadel Press, 2007.

————. *Mind Fist*. Citadel Press, 2008.

————. *Mental Domination*. Citadel Press, 2009.

————. *Mind Assassins*. Citadel Press, 2010.

————. *Mind Warriors*. Citadel Press, 2010.

Lung, Dr. Haha, and Tucker, Eric. *Nine Halls of Death: Ninja Secrets of Mind-Mastery*. Citadel Press, 2007.

Lyman, Stanford M. and Scott, Marvin B. A Sociology of the Absurd, 2nd edition. General Hall, NY, 1989.

Machiavelli, Niccòlo. *The Discourses*. Original trans. Leslie J. Walker. S. J. 1929. Penguin Books, 1998.

————. *The Prince*, 1513 (Misc. translations).

Mahabharata. (Misc. translations).

Musashi, Miyamoto. *Gorin no sho (A Book of Five Rings)*.1645. (Misc. translations).

Norris, Chuck. *The Secret Power Within: Zen Solutions to Real Problems*. Little, Brown and Company, 1998.

Nurariya, Kaitan. *The Religion of the Samurai*. 1913.

Omark, Ralf Dean. *Death on Your Doorstep: 101 Weapons in the Home*. Alpha Publications of Ohio,1995.

Only, Joshua. *Wormwood: The Terrible Truth about Islam.* Only Publications, 2009.

Packard, Vance. *The People Shapers.* Little, Brown, 1977.

Peters, Ralph. *Fighting for the Future.* Stackpole Books, 1999.

Piaget, Gerald W. *Control Freaks: Who They Are and How to Stop Them from Running Your Life.* Doubleday, 1991.

Ratti, Oscar and Westbrook, Adele. *Secrets of the Samurai: The Martial Arts of Feudal Japan.* Tuttle Publishing, 1973.

Ringer, Robert J. *Looking Out for Number One.* Funk & Wagnells, 1977.

————. *Winning Through Intimidation.* Fawcett, 1976.

Sato, Hiroaki. *The Sword and the Mind.* Overlook Press, 1985.

Sawyer, Ralph D. *The Seven Classics of Ancient China.* Basic Books, 1993.

Skinner, Dirk. *Street Ninja: Ancient Secrets for Mastering Today's Mean Streets.* Barricade Books, 1995.

Sohl, Robert and Carr, Audrey. *The Gospel According to Zen.* A Mentor Book, New American Library, 1970.

Suzuki, D.T. *The Awakening of Zen.* Shambhala, 2000.

Suzuki, Shunryu. *Zen Mind, Beginner's Mind.* Shambhala, 2011.

Sun Tzu. *Ping-Fa (The Art of War).* c. 500 B.C. Misc. translations.

Tokitsu, Kenji. *Miyamoto Musashi: His Life and Writings.* Shambala, 2004.

Turnbull, Stephen. *The Samurai and the Sacred.* Osprey, 2006.

Yoda, Hiroka and Alt, Matt. *Ninja Attack: True Tales of Assassins, Samurai, and Outlaws.* Kodansha International, 2010.

Yoritomo, Taishi. *Influence: How to Exert It.* 1916 translation by B. Dangennes. Kissinger Publications.

Yourcenar, Marguerite. *Mishima: A Vision of the Void.* Trans. Alberto Manguel, 1986.

Zen and Shinto: The Story of Japenese Philosophy. Greenwood Press, 1959.

ABOUT THE AUTHOR

Dr. Haha Lung is the author of over two dozen published books on subjects ranging from aberrant anthropology and psychology, martial arts, and mind control. Born in Katmandu, Nepal, a graduate of Ashland University in Ohio, he currently holds degrees in psychology, sociology, math, and science. He currently calls Spirit Lake, Idaho, home.

Other books in Dr. Lung's "Mind Masters" series published by Citadel Press include:

Mind Manipulation (2002)
Mind Control (2006)
Mind Penetration (2007)
Mind Fist (2008)
Mental Dominance (2009)
Mind Assassins (2010)
Mind Warrior (2010)
Ultimate Mind Control (2011)

PREVIOUS DR. LUNG TITLES